Hidden Kingdom

Unveiling the Mysteries of God

Theresa Lorraine

Contents

Introduction

WHAT IS THE HIDDEN KINGDOM OF GOD?

Many of us are familiar with the concept of Heaven.

Many of us were taught to believe in a Heaven that is a far away place, somewhere mysterious we go after we die. Others believe that Heaven is a place that will manifest upon the world after the second coming of Christ. It is a place "out there" or "faraway," of "another future time."

In Buddhism, Hinduism and other forms of Eastern religion, Heaven is a realm we "ascend" to, either by attaining the Buddha state, or by realizing the Tao, or by reaching Liberation, which is a state of spiritual purity. Heaven is thought to be a realm of the immortals and the buddhas, and one must live many lives within samsara, learning lessons through suffering and hardship, before one may ascend to Heaven (or Nirvana, or the Pureland, etc.)

It would seem that every civilization has some concept of Heaven and some way to get there—to that *faraway, someday, future* place.

However, there is a mysterious saying that Christ tells us in the Bible, hinting at the secret nature of Heaven:

" . . . neither will they say, 'Look, here!' or, 'Look, there!' for behold, God's Kingdom is within you." (Luke 17:21)

Some scholars prefer the translation "God's Kingdom is *in your midst*," rather than "within you." Whichever translation is more accurate or was intended two-thousand years ago when Christ was alive, both versions serve the purpose of this book.

Another mysterious saying is revealed by Matt in the Sermon on the Mount: "Blessed are the pure in heart, for they shall see God." (Matt 5:8)

And so by this, we can imagine two mysteries surrounding the spiritual nature of life: first, that Heaven exists as an *immanent* place, not a faraway place; second, that by purifying the heart, we can see God.

The Pure Heart

One of the great mysteries of this Hidden Kingdom of God is a short sentence in the Bible, Matt 5:8, about the "pure heart."

"Blessed are the pure in heart, for they shall see God." (Matt 5:8)

It introduces an important question into Christian practice, and indeed, into the significance of human life: *can we see God?*

Many people of faith deny the experience is possible. Many say it is not scriptural. However, the vision of God has been alive and well in Christianity and other spiritual traditions for thousands of years. In Catholicism, the early church called it the "beatific vision," and it was one of the hallmarks of the saints. Within other religions, this profound experience has been assigned other names, such as *moksha* (Hinduism) or liberation. Receiving the vision of God has been described by hundreds if not thousands of historical figures across civilizations.

This sacred experience is found at the root of every religion; it is at the heart of our knowledge of spiritual life. Without it, we would have little concept of the divine, and mankind's mystical nature would remain unexplored. Not only is it possible to have a personal encounter with the divine, but it is the cornerstone of our spiritual understanding as a species. It is not an event to be pushed to the sidelines, but brought into focus as the central core of religious practice.

Without a personal encounter with the divine, there would be no liberation to be found within religion, only bondage.

And so we should remember that this personal experience of the divine does not come from religion—*it comes from God through you.*

And this is how the nature of the Hidden Kingdom is revealed, which Christ promises us is immanent—within us—around us—existent now.

Heaven is not a faraway place to be entered after death, or at some future appointed time. It is a vision and an experience that many have encountered—a place many have entered even while still alive, through resurrection of the spiritual body. The sheer number of witnesses, continuing from one generation to the next, to this sacred resurrection is what feeds our religious traditions around the world.

And the more people who experience this Heaven, the more hearts are purified, the more people are freed from the bondage of sin and death, the more this spiritual Hidden Kingdom becomes manifest within the material world.

And so this sacred experience of the divine should be honored, preserved, upheld, valued, sought after and restored as the central focus of all religious practice.

The Heart of Sacred Experience

"Experiencing God" and "seeing the divine," due to its inward, subjective nature, can seem like an entry point for delusion and madness within religious practice. For this reason, those who claim to have the ability to "see and hear God" should be observed closely, though respectfully.

Although the revealing of God's Light and Presence during spiritual resurrection *does* happen, it far surpasses what many Christian's term a "conversion experience." Therefore, a person's mental health must always be considered when discussing spiritual encounters.

Many people who suffer from delusions can become convincing spiritual leaders, so we must be cautious and use discernment to separate the wheat from the chaff. God works through all kinds of people, so I am not implying someone with religious delusions cannot also be a wonderful, inspiring and loving person.

However, we should learn to distinguish an encounter with Spirit from our own tendency for self-delusion.

- An encounter of a divine spiritual nature will not lend itself to fear, but result in peace, wisdom, insight, gifts, healing, forgiveness and renewal of the spirit.
- There will be no sense of impending doom or urgency.
- There will be no racing thoughts, no unusual risk taking, grandiosity or ongoing, uncontrollable inner monologue.
- You will hear no voices shouting your name; you will see no physical flashes, shadow figures or imaginary illusions.

- There will be no contact from UFO's or "beings" outside of yourself who exert mental control over you.
- The experience will not be initiated by substances such as psychedelics, drugs, alcohol or other stimulants.

By calling out these distortions of the mind, I wish to draw our attention away from the imaginative and focus purely on the sacred.

So then, if not anything like the list above, what is the sacred experience at the heart of all religion?

In Catholicism, we have the incredible account of this experience by St. Augustine of Hippo in his autobiography, "Confessions."

St. Augustine sought to know the nature of evil, and asked a question that might be familiar to all of us: "If God is so good, why is there so much evil in the world?"

During a moment of deep inward meditation, he encountered the Spirit. God answered his question by revealing His nature to St. Augustine. The saint's description begins with the famous words,

". . . I entered into my inward Self, You being my Guide: I was able to do this, because You became my Helper.

I entered and beheld with the eye of my soul (such as it was), above the same eye of my soul, above my mind, the **Light** **Unchangeable**. . . .

He that knows the Truth, knows what that **Light** is; and he that knows It, knows eternity.

Love knows it. O Truth Who are Eternity! and Love Who are Truth! and Eternity Who are Love! You are my God, to You do I sigh night and day. You when I first knew, You lifted me up, that I might see what I might see, and yet could not comprehend. And You beat back the weakness of my sight, streaming forth Your beams of light upon me most strongly, and I trembled with love and awe: and I perceived myself to be far off from You, in the region of unlikeness, as if I heard Your voice from on high: "I am the food of grown men. Grow, and you shall feed upon Me; you will not digest Me, like how food is digested into your body, but you shall be converted into Me."

This sacred experience of encountering God fills an entire chapter in St. Augustine's autobiography, and it's well worth reading for anyone interested in the subject of divine revelation or enlightenment. This powerful description of the beatific vision happened around 400 C.E. This vision is a hallmark of all saints, shamans, gurus and illumined souls from various different spiritual traditions.

In the vast practice of Hinduism, narrowing upon the branch of Vedanta, we find a similar description of a divine encounter in the Gospel of Sri Ramakrishna, where he experienced the vision of Mother Kali around 1856. Kali was the embodiment of the mother goddess he worshiped at a temple where he served as a priest. In The Gospel of Sri Ramakrishna, his description is as follows:

. . . in my heart of hearts, there was flowing a current of intense bliss, never experienced before, and I had the immediate knowledge of the Light that was Mother.... It was as if houses, doors, temples and all other things vanished altogether; as if there was nothing anywhere; And what I saw was a boundless infinite Conscious sea of Light! . . . (continued from a

separate page) within me there was a steady flow of undiluted bliss, altogether new, and I felt the presence of the Divine Mother."

Here, although heralding from two different holy traditions, we see a very similar experience emerge, lending itself to divine instruction and insight.

This experience also appears in Buddhism and Taoism. In Taoist legend, such figures are called "Real People" and are thought to be immortal, because they are known to appear even after death in dreams and visions to help guide others toward the "attainment of the Tao."

These so-called "real people" are seen with a halo of light around them . . . a certain illumination.

This description of holy Light through encountering God is common throughout the world, though it can be obscured by differences in language, religious doctrine, mythology and culture.

A few of the common traits between enlightenment experiences are as follows:

- *seeing the primordial Light of Consciousness or Spirit as an ocean around us;*
- *discovering the presence of the Divine within the heart;*
- *permanent transformation, illumination and resurrection of the spiritual body;*
- *feeling the Divine Companion enter into the body, becoming One;*
- *joy, higher Love, or in the paraphrased words of Ramakrishna, "immediate knowledge . . . undiluted bliss, altogether new . . . and the [divine] presence."*
- *a superconscious understanding of the unitive nature of Reality, or as I call it in this book, "the Hidden Kingdom of God."*
- *lending itself to a writable, recountable understanding of the divine that lends itself to the renewal of doctrine.*

This last point, I cannot stress enough. A godly encounter will lend itself to a writable, recountable understanding of the divine that lends itself to the renewal of doctrine. Although the experience of the divine has a profound impact on any man or woman who encounters it, with elements completely beyond our capacity to express, the knowledge gained by this unveiling of the holy Light lends itself to a legible, coherent and relevant understanding of the spiritual nature of things—a window into this Hidden Kingdom of the Heart.

It is not just "a feeling" or "a moment." It is a hard event imbued with knowledge, resurrection, and a higher spiritual Love that illuminates the whole body.

The Light Unchangeable

St. Augustine of Hippo describes, "I entered and beheld with the eye of my soul (such as it was), above the same eye of my soul, above my mind, the Light Unchangeable. . . . "

Just as Sri Ramakrishna states, "I had immediate knowledge of the Light that was Mother."

This Light Unchangeable is experienced within us when we come into union with the divine. This state of union does not change or waver; a bar of light is known to pervade the body, centered upon the heart, which lends superconscious knowledge to the mind.

From this merging with the Spirit of God, the Hidden Kingdom is revealed. From that moment on, Heaven is seen to be immanent, and the great mysteries of Life are known. We dwell from that day forward in the Presence of God.

It is all through the revealed, pure heart.

And this is the greatest mystery across all religious traditions—this mystery of the pure heart.

The Sacred Experience
CAN YOU SEE GOD?

What right would I have to speak of the Hidden Kingdom, without my own encounter of the divine Light?

There is no greater joy than knowing God.

I ask that the Lord of Love work through me to write in purity, using the gifts He has given me to express the inexpressible, speak the unspeakable, describe the indescribable, and glorify the Name of All: "I AM."

May this Work be for the liberation and salvation of souls.

The Transformative Power of Death

Leading up to this experience of the divine Light at the tender age of twelve years old, my mother was dying from breast cancer. It was during this very great trial that I awakened to the Presence of God.

Prior to this experience, I was an average child. I had one sibling, an older brother, who was a typical boy who excelled at sports, loved video games, and constantly teased me. I had many friends at school, was well-liked by my teachers, very sociable, enjoyed reading all sorts of books, playing piano, taking singing and ballet lessons, and spending my time outdoors. I had a black cat named Midnight who was my very good friend. I grew up in the Pacific Northwest, in Washington State, the land of blackberry blossoms and evergreen trees, roaring rivers and soaring mountains. A place of beauty and ruggedness where I spent a good amount of time in the woods.

However, when my mother became ill, everything changed. Due to my father's work in the music industry, we moved from the beautiful Pacific Northwest to the arid cityscape of Los Angeles, which meant leaving behind my best friends, my beloved forests and everything I'd known of life up to that point.

Entering a new public school was difficult. I didn't have my usual group of friends around me for support.

The sudden isolation compounded my grief, as my mother grew more and more sick, until she passed away in March of the year 2000. And this is truly where my trial began.

An Atheist Upbringing

I think it's important to note that I was raised in an atheist household. So when those important conversations began to happen surrounding my mother's death, such as *"What happens to Mom after she dies?"*, my father, who was a wonderful man and a staunch atheist, told me, "When we die, we disappear and return to nature. *We become nothing.*"

Interestingly enough, this concept of emptiness, of returning to nothing, is found in some branches of Buddhism. It's this idea that beyond the impermanence of natural phenomena, beyond these waves of cause-and-effect that we call karma, resides a sort of "empty field of potential," *a void,* they say, which is very mysterious and intriguing. I love this idea of a void that is also full of potential. It's very mind-boggling, and I think that's part of the beauty of it.

And so that's what my father told me, essentially, that when we die, we return to the "Void of Nature." *We become nothing. And that was that.*

My father was not a Buddhist. And yet, fortunately for me, atheism and some branches of Buddhism have this belief in common. It meant that I didn't have a story or a narrative to cling to, which would help soothe my wounded child's ego. My mother had died, and the explanation was, well, *no explanation at all.*

And before you get the wrong idea, my father was a very kind and honorable man. He was an older parent. He was forty-five years old when I was born. He was an accomplished musician, an academic and a teacher. He lived by his virtues, a master of karma yoga, you might say.

The Importance of Virtue

And I think this, too, is significant. Because we weren't just an atheist family: we were a virtuous family. There was a sense of chivalry and honor in everything we did, almost like a knighthood.

Virtue corresponds with *pure-heartedness*.

We were an atheist family, but we lived by a code:

- do good for the sake of good,
- treat others the way you want to be treated,
- always be a peacemaker,
- never hold grudges,
- always forgive,
- pursue your passions in life,
- don't live for money,
- be on good terms with all people,
- don't let another's actions be an excuse for your own,
- do the right thing because it's *who you are*.

My father was a great lover of wisdom, particularly Greek philosophy. He lived by his ideals, and he raised us the same way.

As I've gotten older, I sometimes wonder at the immense blessing it was to be raised in an atheist family. My father taught us that *if something exists, there must be proof.* So I knew early on that if God exists, He was to be seen. Face-to-face.

The Fire of Self-Reflection

But I digress. In the wake of my mother's death, as I was grappling with the concept of my own mortality, my father told me that after we die, we become nothing. It was very difficult for me at twelve years old to imagine becoming nothing, as I'm sure it must be difficult for us at any age. It was a little frightening. It was my first time confronting my own mortality, and I spent a lot of time thinking about it. It was both a blessing and a curse that we had recently moved 2000 miles away from my old town, and I didn't have many new friends to distract me from my quandary.

My mother's death lit a fire in me. I needed to make sense of what had happened to her, and I needed to integrate the loss of her and the experience of grief into my psyche somehow. But my father's atheist explanation and my family's beliefs did not allow me to have any comforting story of Heaven or an afterlife. Instead, I was left chasing my tail with endless questions.

I would spend my time at school sitting quietly out on the quad, observing my classmates, and wondering at our fate.

Could it be that someday, *everything* would become *nothing?*

How was that possible?

How could it be that my mother, who I loved so much, was gone forever? And as importantly, what would happen to me after *I* died? Would *I* become nothing and cease to exist?

How could I ever stop existing if I exist now?

But I could not deny that my mother had died and she appeared to be totally gone. I saw no evidence of God or gods in the world. So then, if people die and become nothing, what about *me* is real? Why does any of this exist? How can it exist, if it becomes *nothing?*

I know. Deep thoughts for a twelve year old. And to clarify, I was not suicidal. I did not want to die. But I was experiencing an existential crisis and I needed resolution.

Upon reflection, if my father had been Christian and if I had been raised in a church where I could speak to pastors and other adults who had faith, this experience of seeing God face-to-face might not have happened to me, because maybe I would have accepted that the Bible was the final word on God and there was nothing else to find. I would have been told my mother went to Heaven, and to have blind faith in Jesus, and maybe that would have satisfied me.

But that was not the case living in an atheist home, where religion was not taken seriously at all, and the Bible held no authority to me.

Instead, when my mother passed away, I was left with this great gaping hole of confusion. I was seeking validity of my own existence and whether anything survived after death. And this was closely intertwined with whether or not God existed. The two questions seemed inextricably linked. If I could find the answer to one, I would have the answer to the other.

But the Bible was not enough. *I needed proof. I needed evidence.* If God exists, if anything eternal and perfect and True exists in this life, then show me. *I must see Him.*

The Practice of "Neti, Neti"

And lo and behold, without realizing it, I began to practice what the Buddhists call *"neti, neti,"* and this is the practice of breaking down the ego by identifying what it is not. And it doesn't have to happen in meditation. You can do this every day, all day long, if you're brave enough (*or, at least, as brave as a twelve-year-old.*)

I will admit I was a bit obsessive. My mind had found a problem, a logical fallacy hidden within the fabric of myself, the biggest question we ask ourselves about life, and I could not have peace until I had an answer.

So the question was, *"Who am I? What about me is real?"* And anytime I examined a part of myself, wondering if it would exist after death, what I found was, *"No, not this."*

Is my physical body who I am? *No, not if it dies and becomes nothing.*

Am I my mother's daughter? *No, not if I die and become nothing.*

Is my creativity who I am? *No, not if I die and become nothing.*

Am I my bloodline or my heritage? *No, not if I die and become nothing.*

Am I my name or the color of my eyes? *No, not if I die and become nothing.*

Am I my interests? My talents? My possessions? What about my favorite subjects in school? *No, I can't be any of these, because I will die and become nothing.*

I could find nothing about myself that was real, nothing about myself that would survive death, for as I had seen with my mother, nothing seemed to have survived.

The longer this went on, the more hopeless I felt.

I became more obsessed with finding the answer to whether or not God existed. I argued ceaselessly with friends and family over the existence of God. One day I believed, the next day I didn't. I was at war with myself, and I was deeply distraught. Truly, it seemed that nothing in this world was real.

Ego Death

And all of this culminated into an incredible moment in my bedroom where the internal walls of myself began to crumble. I was at the tail end of 7th grade. I remember I was sitting on my bedroom floor. It was the weekend, sunny outside, about late morning, the house was empty, and I was reading a book about Celtic mythology. I specifically remember the book, because in my frustration at people's lack of ability to answer my questions about God, I had taken to reading various different books about ancient belief systems, some of which were more occult or mythological in nature, looking for an answer that would satisfy *the terrible fire in my head.*

But for several weeks leading up to this point, I had been plagued by a growing sense of guilt. I remember I couldn't focus on what I was reading, because I was so consumed by this inner turmoil.

I was beginning to suspect that I was accountable for my own inability to know God.

I was at fault.

Who else could I blame, but me?

I needed God at any cost, but I didn't even know what that meant, just that a burning emptiness had taken up my heart that nothing could soothe, and thoughts of God filled my mind every day, and a deep, terrible yearning I could not explain.

I had cried and begged and prayed for God to give me some sign of "His" existence. Nothing answered, and yet this agony and yearning remained. I began to suspect . . . maybe it was *my own fault.*

Maybe *I was accountable* for not being able to solve this mystery.

Maybe I had some shortcoming, some fatal flaw that stood between me and God, preventing Him from finding me, or Me from finding Him.

A great wave of grief swelled through me—such desolation and hopelessness. I have never been in such a dark place. I felt a great and terrible cavern of emptiness open inside of me, and instead of fighting against it, I let go.

I fell down into that darkness at the heart of myself.

I knew that if I hit the bottom of the hole, I would die, I would shatter and cease to exist. I felt the last shreds of myself beginning to crumble. And instead of fighting it, I plunged straight in. I let go of my pride. I surrendered.

With all my grief and despair, I cried out from my heart of hearts—

"God, I'm sorry! Please forgive me! I need you!"

The Body Becomes Light

At that moment, I felt struck by lightning. I felt every cell in my body change and become Light.

There was no physical flash, but I felt Light strike me, pouring down from above and permeating my whole body. I felt my heart ignite like the Sun. A great wave of love and purity swept through me, so powerful that I couldn't breathe. I felt my heart exploding, my body straining to contain it.

I dissolved into Love itself.

Then, like a silent gong being struck, a great vibration enveloped me, very high and very pure, not heard through the ears but *through my essence or soul,* of which I was unaware of and blind to before that moment.

Every atom in existence resonated with the words, *I AM!*

I became submerged within an immense Presence, a Person, a Spirit, a Consciousness that interconnected and pervaded everything around me. Everything became One. *It was so big, and so right, and so perfect. It was pure*—I didn't understand purity before that moment. But I recognized this Presence—I knew Him instantly—I *remembered* Him, for how could I not? I knew this Love had been with me for all eternity, and *I remembered what eternity meant within this Love.*

I became aware of *my eternal Self.*

It was like someone had turned the lights on in the room, and I could see it clearly for the first time. God was everywhere. Like music with no sound, everything was vibrating with this purity, Light, connection and Presence, "*I AM.*"

Immense Love filled me of a kind I cannot explain—Love so powerful, I felt myself destroyed utterly and absolutely, and then reborn into a new sense of myself, resurrected within this Love, my body filled to the brim with Light and Spirit and Knowledge of God, my sense of self utterly decimated and born anew. I saw the old "me," absent and empty of this Love, burn away like ashes—*she was never real. She never existed.*

And I felt within me a Light and a Power and a Joy that was Creation itself.

Nothing can truly exist apart from this Love, *for this Love is Life itself.*

Knowing God is truly knowing ourselves.

We can only become real within His Light. All else is mere shadow.

Everything that had been empty and strange and confusing before, was suddenly illuminated in perfect clarity. And I felt that I had come home.

Remembering, Not Discovering

Around, within, throughout me was God. His Presence was not new—*I remembered Him instantly*. I remembered this Presence more clearly than I could recognize my own face. God's spirit appeared to me as a great, vibrating ocean of Consciousness and primordial Light—much finer and more beautiful than sunlight—and I knew Him as though I had always known Him. I wondered how I could have forgotten the most obvious and essential thing about existence— *Of course, God! How could I forget God? Here He Is! He is this! The Light that gave birth to light: the Light upon which light rests. We are all within Him, and He within Us, and the two are One. He is Love that gave birth to love, Life that gave birth to life, Wisdom and Truth and Beauty and Essence that is beyond me and yet all of me, for I am His, and He is Mine.*

There exists no greater Friend, no greater joy than the remembrance of that Friendship. My heart came alive, and that Life was Joy.

His Light was within me, and I saw that *I did not exist but for Him*. Through infinite layers of existence, I felt dimensions open within me, around me, and I saw that all levels of all things were pervaded and connected by One Spirit: the Truth, the Love, the Reality.

One God, One Spirit, One Self, One Creation, One Existence. One.

All Things Seen as One

I remember staring at my bedpost, the desk, the wall. I remember crawling across the floor and touching my nightstand, surprised that my hand didn't pass straight through it, that the nightstand was still solid. This Presence was so powerful, so vital and pure and true, it made the physical world seem porous by comparison; physical matter was a mere plastic facade, and this omniscient force was true Reality.

I remember that I stood up and walked through my house into the living room, with a sense that I was walking through this vast ocean of Spirit. God's presence was everywhere, vibrating and resonating within everything. His Light, through the heart, made all things beautiful. I sat down on the couch and I looked outside the window, and another wave struck me, as I saw the sky, the earth, the trees, and felt an intense *connection* between everything. It was all One.

I saw how God's Spirit pervaded everything. It was in my own heart and mind, and in the world around me, all of us interconnected by this great Love and Light and Life and Consciousness.

Before I had been blind, and now I could truly *see*.

It says in the Qur'an, *"He is the listening in the ears and the seeing through the eyes,"* and this is true. I felt God within me, closer than my own heartbeat. He was my "I," and I was perceiving the "I" through the "I."

You must become One with God in order to see Him and perceive Him like this.

His Spirit comes into you, and dwells within you, and then all of His knowledge is illuminated within your inward Self.

God Dwells In the Pure Heart

Now I knew that God dwelled in my heart, for I could feel His presence throughout my whole body like a shining light. Centered on the heart, this pure and perfect Love glowed like the Sun. And I knew my heart to be infinite, for it contained God Himself, and God was infinite, and I knew what infinity meant, for I too was Infinite and Eternal, which goes beyond the concept of human imagination.

I remembered this Love had been with me since the *beginning of beginnings*; throughout vast expanses of time and space, this love had always been with me. *Eternity feels like all power contained within an instant; knowledge preserved outside of Time; without the cloudiness of memory, perceived clearly, everything is real and now.*

In the power of this light of pure Consciousness, I felt my old identity fall off me like dead skin. I felt like she had never been alive. Never existed. Now, I existed for the first time, and this "Me" was Life itself, and Life meant unity, purity, knowledge and Truth.

In God and in Heaven, all things are known and perceived *through the pure heart.*

God's Consciousness is Light

I saw that God is Perfect Consciousness (or "pure Spirit.") That Consciousness is not contained in the brain, but exists as a part of nature, a universal law, harmonizing and vibrating within all things, and we are submerged within Consciousness like an ocean. This ocean is *Absolute*. It is *Pristine*. It is *Light*. But it's not the kind of light we see with our eyes from the sun. The light from the sun can barely be called light, because it is harsh and destructive, it burns, and it only illuminates the physical world.

But the light of God permeates everything, including the Spirit; it is both internal and external; it is pleasing to the spiritual eyes. It is seen through the heart and illuminates everything with knowledge. It does not burn, but gives Life and Order to all things.

This light is Beauty itself, and it made all things beautiful and perfect as they were, and I saw that this Light was what I belonged to, that it filled my heart, mind and body just as it filled the room. *It was the Life of my life and the Soul of my soul. My Creator, My Source, My Sustainer, this Love that had been with me and was for me since the beginning of beginnings.* And this is God.

God's Consciousness is Love

I saw that God is Love. But not the kind of love we experience as human beings. Human love can barely be called love, because human love wounds us. God's Love is *the power of creation itself.* It is a Power. It is pure; it is life-sustaining, impartial, the backbone of Reality, the immortal essence hidden within all things; the great harmonizing force of the cosmos, the great Song of Being. And I knew the true heart of my existence was only Love.

That Love became me, for when we become One with God, His Love and pure nature lives within us as His Children.

The Acorn and the Oak Tree

I knew the root of my "I" was God Himself, because He showed me. And yet I perceived some sense of distance between us, like an acorn gazing up at an oak tree. I knew that although all things were One, yet somehow I existed on a plane slightly removed from His Perfection—that He was the Father, and I was the child.

And I remember the craving in my heart as I gazed upon this pure and perfect Consciousness. "I must become That," I thought, even as I knew it to be an impossible task, for who could be as great as God? How could such a little acorn become such a giant oak tree?

And then I heard the words pass through me in a wave: "*You Must Try.*" Those were the first words He spoke to me. The command resonated through my heart. And although the words were few, the meaning was great, and imbued with knowledge and layers of information several leagues deep, and far too intricate to explain through the English language. I knew so much more than I could ever put into words.

I knew I had come into this life for the purpose of serving Him—that I'd sought after Him for all eternity—and I yearned to emulate His perfection. I yearned *to serve*; by serving we become like Him. By imitating His perfect Love, I, too, would resonate and harmonize and grow into Him, and that's what I yearned to be: One. All things harmonizing to One.

And I knew the bar by which all things were measured: it was His Spirit of Loving Purity. By merging with this ocean of Love, I had found the pure root of myself, and so I knew every law of the Spirit, for it was Myself *in the most highest and humbling sense*: a Self that did not belong to me individually, but the same Self or Spirit shared by all Life, to be honored and known as the true Sacred.

I saw how all spiritual law followed the attributes of this Pure Consciousness: all of life emulating and reaching for the Father. I could see it all laid out before me plainly. We are not complete by ourselves; only in Him do we become whole.

By knowing God's Presence, I had been given the keys to the Hidden Kingdom, and all of the knowledge of spiritual law was illuminated within my own consciousness. I had become, by His grace, *purehearted.*

We exist in blindness, stumbling through the trials of our lives, only to eventually master what is, in fact, the practice of perfect Love: to realize the mirror of the world, to cease harming and injuring others through our own ignorance, and live in harmony with all life. This is truly how we honor God, for God resides within all things, and what we do to another, we do to ourselves.

Indeed, His Spirit IS *everything. And I do mean everything. There is nothing that is not God.*

That's why we are to act as peacemakers.

We've been darting around this Universe for a very long time, and our soul's purpose is to integrate all attributes of divine Love into our Being, *that we might shine like Him.*

We are to become like Him, the only Truth. We are to become Divine Love.

The seed is to grow into the Tree.

The Divine Task

I sensed that I had reached the end of things, as it were. I felt like Dorothy in the Wizard of Oz. I had looked behind the red curtain, I had seen what there was to see, and now I knew it within my sacred heart, so I could find it anywhere, in any life, in any world. I knew that We could not be separated, for I had been resurrected in His Spirit, granted His presence by grace, and now He was my "I" and my Everything.

And I wondered what I was to do next, since I felt like I had reached the pinnacle of things, for what else had I to learn, what could be greater than God?

And God answered my question again, without me having to ask, for God lives in our heart of hearts. He said, "*Save them.*"

The command moved through me in a wave, and I understood God had a great Task for me; that I had been given a great treasure and I must share it with others; that I was to gather up souls in His net of knowledge and guide them to the truth within themselves. He wanted to be known by His children— He wanted me to share my Salvation with others. I knew this was my purpose, my calling and my mission. Yet I was only twelve years old. It seemed like a great mountain lay before me, for I could not fathom how God would help me in this Work, or how I was to share His Love with others, or make them see this hidden greatness within themselves and within the world. Who would believe me?

God does not hide Himself because He is deceptive—we fail to see Him because we are so small. The fault lies within us, not within Him.

I was not afraid. I was very happy that God had a Task for me to fulfill and Work for me to do—Work that would make a life worth living. I was eager to serve Him in this way, for I felt I owed Him a great debt—the debt of Love—the debt of my Life, of my very existence. I had been given a great love of the world, and a great love for all things sacred and True, and I deeply wanted to give this love to everyone.

After the Vision

When I saw my father later that evening, I was struck that I could see myself within him. *His heart was my own, for his heart was contained within my own, for I contained God within my heart, and God is infinite.* And this is a great mystery, how the heart is infinite while the body is so finite, and yet that is the reality of the Hidden Kingdom: although we appear as tiny physical bodies, the heart is truly infinite and contains everything.

And from that day forward, I could feel people's thoughts and intentions through my heart, because there no longer seemed to be any boundary between us. I saw that they were in me and I was in them, and through God we all shared the same Spirit.

Changes to Mind, Self and Character

In the days and weeks that followed, the vision of God's beauteous light faded from the world around me and took up home within me; meaning, I felt His light and His spirit throughout my whole body, and His presence remained ever in my heart like a glowing Sun. His knowledge remained within me, for it was my "I," and I found that I could see the Truth in things like I couldn't before.

I no longer wanted to cut flowers from the garden, for I knew God's Spirit resided within them, and I didn't want to interrupt God's work within the flower.

Knowing that God's spirit pervaded all things, I understood that worshiping a rock was the same as worshiping the statue of a saint. Giving a bowl of water to a dog was the same as giving money to a church, for God's spirit resided within both.

The world became my temple, and life itself was my religion. And indeed, I had no specific desire or need for a church or a religion, for I knew God's presence directly. I saw my life as a spiritual life. His pure light inspires Wisdom, peace and great patience within us.

I became very calm and tranquil, and no matter the trials of life, I always felt a deep sense of peace, as my heart knew its home. There was no longer any inner struggle, no wrong sense of myself, no confusion or shakiness. I knew who I was, and with that certainty came a great peace, calmness and focus.

My atheist family did not really believe my experience, no matter how hard I tried to explain it to them. My Christian aunts and relatives were surprised to hear about it, but I was still very young, and so they didn't ask me many questions. I think they thought it was all within my childhood imagination. I think perhaps now, many years after the fact, they believe me more than they did back then, seeing that my faith has not wavered. I speak of God happily and often, with great love and personal intimacy, as though discussing a shared friend. I am always eager to talk about Him, as it inspires deep joy in my heart.

Just as a parent cannot stop speaking of their child, because it inspires so much joy within them, so I could not stop speaking or thinking of God, as the reminder of that Love inspired so much joy within me.

When I did selfless and compassionate things, in the mindset of highest Love, I felt the glow of God's spirit brighten within my body. My heart filled with Love and indescribable joy, and I was lifted into a wondrous state of happiness. If I was ever sad, I only had to do something kind and selfless and good, and I would feel God's joy lift me again. And in truth, I never really became sad like I had before, for my heart was not empty but filled with God's love, which is joy itself. I saw the world through eyes filled with purpose and wonder. I could not remain trapped by gloomy thoughts for long.

When I focused on the memory of my Enlightenment, I would see it all over again, and I would cry, overwhelmed by the deep love and devotion I felt for God. My heart yearned to serve Him in everything that I did, and in all things, I only desired closeness with Him. I understood that this Love carried supernatural Power—it was the will of Life itself.

It's all One: Spirit, Love, Truth, Knowledge, Life. In language, they are five things, but in God, they are One.

Sometimes that Spirit would pick me up in a wave and send me soaring so high that I started laughing and laughing. And in silence and solitude, I would sink into this deep oasis inside of myself, an immense and bottomless peace and silence, where the Presence of God glowed within my heart. I found within me the ability to sit quietly for hours, focused on that inner joy of being, and there was great relief in my soul during those periods of silence, for the soul yearns for this quiet solitude and deep companionship with Her Lord.

Gifts of the Spirit

Once the heart is aglow with Truth, you are content to be anywhere, doing anything, for you take God with you wherever you go, and whatever you do, *you are in Heaven.*

And I felt a new power of the Spirit within my body. I channeled it into playing the piano, writing poetry and novels. I developed a quick sense of humor, a cheerfulness and a friendliness toward everyone. I finished writing a four-hundred page book by the time I was thirteen, many hundreds of poems, and I wrote dozens of piano pieces. There seemed to be no end to my creativity, and it brought me such joy to do these things with God.

I also began to receive very vivid dreams, filled with visions, premonitions, knowledge, insights, poetry and music, that have continued to this day. Much knowledge has been imparted to me through dreams and sudden visions of this *hidden, spiritual Kingdom* in which we dwell.

I gained an ability to know when people were lying to me. It was as though I could hear the lie in their words when they spoke, at times knowing their thoughts before they shared them. I knew all of this through our shared heart. I've been asked many times by close friends and family whether or not I can read their mind. Jokingly, of course, for in the West, people don't truly believe in these things. But at times, I can. This is because the Holy Spirit is shared between all people, so when the Spirit is realized and we are resurrected by God's grace, we receive special insights as well. Although I am not a trained theologian, in Christianity, I believe this is called the *body of Christ*. It is much more than simply "the church"—it is a spiritual body that exists in union with the Holy Spirit, and therefore we become interconnected with all life.

My purpose in sharing these changes in my character is not to boast (except perhaps to boast of God's greatness, for His gifts are numerous and without end,) but to demonstrate how, through this experience, I received immense psychological and physical healing, inner peace, wholeness, compassion, confidence, talent, giftedness, detachment, inspiration, insight and wisdom. Through this experience I came into myself, and I witnessed the true nature of Love.

So this is not a mental health issue or a delusion. It is something else entirely.

Turning Away from Childish Things

Some changes to my character were more like a "turning away" from childhood things.

I found the worship of fame and materialism to cause a great sense of dissonance within my heart. I lost interest in collecting toys, watching mindless cartoons or other programming on TV, because I saw no Truth in it. I also did not develop any interest in watching religious programming. Much of our modern mainstream religion neglects these deep spiritual truths.

Instead, I gravitated toward storytelling that struck upon the heart of our humanity: wholesome tales of virtue, heroism, courage and ascension.

I saw instantly that our society seemed to exist in opposition to the Truth of God's nature, remaining oblivious to these higher realms of life within the Spirit. I saw glorification of war and violence, base objectification of women, and worship of fame and materialism. I saw how this corruption in our society's values lent itself to needless suffering, creating a layer of ignorance and blindness over our hearts like a suffocating mask of delusion. It caused a great sense of unrest in my spirit.

Likewise, although I read extensively, I did not remain long in the so-called "New Age" movement of psychics, mediums, aura readers, spirit guides and near death experiences, for although I saw some elements of the sacred contained within these things, nothing compared to the experience of God firsthand. I had no interest in contacting ghosts, developing special "magic" powers, working spells or any such nonsense. I saw that all things were contained within God and known through God, and so God alone is the final summit and the goal of life.

Yet I also saw how rigid religious thinking created a barrier between the mind and the pure heart. Religious thinking is the same no matter the specific tradition: it is dogmatic and narrow, and it stifles creativity and expression. I saw only hypocrisy and fear within religiosity, Bible worship and the cry of salesman-like Salvation promises. This, too, fails to glorify God's true nature of Love.

Whatever we practice, it cannot be a performative faith.

All things must be done through the heart. And the heart must be continually deepened.

The answer to developing an authentic, spiritual and healthful society truly seems to be the Middle Way— living within the world but not of the world— remaining true to our virtues while graciously enjoying our freedom within God's loving embrace.

Detachment and Contentment

Inever fully came to identify with my physical body—I knew the truth of myself in a spiritual sense, *as an essence and a power and a thriving Life within*—and so I saw my body as simply a vessel and a tool for God's work, and my gender as simply a performative mask, hiding the formless and transcendent soul within. That is to say, I never questioned whether I was a girl or a boy, I was content with myself, but I simply didn't bother with such ponderings as they didn't seem important. The body dies, but within God, my essence is eternal.

I experienced what I might call romantic love or "crushes," yet the physical urges often associated with romantic love seemed dampened within me. I had little carnal sense. I was more interested in pursuing my spirituality than pursuing relationships, for within God *there are far higher pleasures to be experienced within the Spirit,* pleasures that do not age or sicken the body, but that lend themselves to longevity and joy.

That being said, I never shied away from relationships with people. I enjoyed companionship, and I have to say, I was not very discerning in my early years. I fell into friendship with all sorts of different groups of people. At times, I felt myself in love with everyone, and yet I rarely experienced lust. I believe I was in love with the glimmer of God within them.

To everyday things, I became very easygoing and impartial, to the extent that it was difficult to feel like I had any preferences at all. *God's wholeness negated everything.* Nothing seemed lacking. I felt no desire for material things. I knew myself, and in that knowledge was a deep wholeness, a joy and peace beyond measure. I had discovered within myself a holiness and a Truth that was more beautiful and transcendent and incredible than anything this world could offer. *I was in constant awe.* Laughter came easily. Everything I did, I did for God, with God, in God.

At the very mention of spiritual things, my heart would leap and I would talk someone's ear off, eager to speak of the thing I loved the most—kind of like I'm talking your ear off now! It was like a fountain of knowledge would pour out of me that I couldn't contain. People would ask me where I had learned such things, as I was still very young, and I couldn't answer them, because God's Truth lived within me as a glowing light, and how could I describe such a wellspring of life and knowledge that dwelled in my Heart?

The Difference Between God and Religion

I quickly learned that people who followed a religion, much to my initial confusion, did not seem to know God in this way, internally, from the heart, as Self, as the "I," for they had not seen Him.

And so I learned that when I said "God," my concept came from this pure experience, while when other people said "God," their concept came from books or religious teachings.

And yet there was a lot of overlap, because religions are founded upon this kind of truth and understanding. At first, it was confusing and nuanced, as the truth would draw me close, yet the dissonance of miscomprehension or mispractice would push me away.

Whereas I thought of God as the root of myself, as Love and unity and purity, "believers" or "seekers" typically thought of God as separate from themselves or outside of themselves, some transcendent force untouchable or unreachable by us mere mortal earthlings.

Which of course is not true, for God resides within you.

And I came to realize that actually, the struggle of mankind to comprehend God is *the opposite* of what most people might think. It's *easy* to imagine a distant creator God, an abstract "divine essence" relegated to theories, philosophy or marginalia, enthroned somewhere in a distant concept of Heaven, far removed to some "other" time and place.

Likewise, it's easy to imagine God as simply "nature" or "the Universe," passively cycling away without any bother for anyone.

It is very, *very* difficult for mankind to comprehend how *close* God truly is to us, how *everything in our lives* is held within and manifested through that Great Spirit, and yet how *totally invisible and undetectable* He remains, until the spiritual eyes are opened.

Truly, He is beyond the comprehension of the intellect.

So I came to think of religious people and atheists as one and the same, for before the vision of God, everything is in darkness, and after the vision of God, everything is illuminated.

Prior to this experience, you see God through the eyes of religion.

After this experience, you see religion through the eyes of God.

Which sounds very impressive and fancy, but truly, is no great feat once He is seen. Then His companionship becomes as unquestionable as gravity and as normal as breathing.

So, with this in mind, I had no great need for a church, for I dwelled within the holiest of holy places—the pure heart.

And yet, because I loved to worship, I would find myself in a church, or a temple, or any holy place of spiritual practice, singing hymns and praising God with those around me.

It took a long time for me to differentiate between the many various branches of religions, as it all seemed irrelevant to me after this experience. I can't say I'm very good at remembering the nuanced differences between schools of thought. My mind tends to focus on unity rather than splitting hairs between doctrines. Wherever I see God, I point it out, and that's about as complicated as I get.

The true nature of the heart can only be understood by those who have known it themselves, but I will try to explain: the heart, although centered within the body as a glowing Sun, is boundless and within everything. Once pure, all things are known to be held within the heart, and the heart is known to be infinite. Once the true nature of the heart becomes illuminated, we reside within the Truth and all things become sacred.

Once God is seen within the heart, God is seen throughout the world. *As within, so without.*

As Jesus says, the body is the temple, and Heaven is within you.

We are in the midst of a Hidden Kingdom, and we can't even see it.

Friendship and Companionship

As you might imagine, not many people are aware of divine things. So around some groups of people, I felt lonely, but with God, I was never alone. I took comfort in reading spiritual books about the lives of those who had had similar experiences. True friendship is the shared spirit of God, and so I found deep friendship with those of virtuous hearts of selfless service and humility.

The character of a person denotes their purity of heart—not necessarily what they profess with their mouths, but how they live their lives. Therefore, my friends came from many varied religious backgrounds; many were agnostic, but all were kind, loving and soft-hearted people. I did not shy away from atheists, or people of any variety of faith, for I saw it all as the same thing. *Either the light is on, or the light is off.*

Either one has had the vision, or one has not.

You can tell when one has had the vision, for their heart is different, their joy is different, their character is pure, they love to speak of holy things, and they cry true tears of joy and emotion when they speak of God. They have deep intimacy with Him, and it shows in their love of people and careful consideration of spiritual things. Because they are not blind to God's presence, they consider God's nature in everything that they do.

That is not to say we do not suffer. God's children suffer greatly at times—a good life is full of trials and triumphs, and suffering reveals the true power of the soul—yet we are granted His protection in all things.

So although I did not boast and was not hard-nosed about it, I always looked for opportunities to encourage the faith and spirituality of others.

And of course, I loved everyone, and blamed no one, because God lives within everyone, and so to love God is to love all people, and our love must be impartial and unconditional for it to be Pure.

We cannot love people if we only look at what they do to others, because people are consumed by an unintentional sort of self-preoccupation, a naive selfishness, and therefore incomplete by design.

Through some trials and minor heartbreaks, I learned that you should always expect people to do the opposite of what is good, because all goodness comes from God. And you should always expect people to fail at every task, because success is only granted by God. I do not mean to be callous or rude, but rather, by remembering our human limitations, *let us free ourselves to love deeply. We can love people much more easily if we simply expect them to behave as people.*

I mean to say that, unless one walks closely with God and has a character of great virtue or is very blessed, *it is hard to be good.* But that is no excuse not to love people.

It's good to have no expectations of anyone, to help everyone as much as you can, and be delighted in even the smallest Good that people do. Even the smallest good is a glimmer of God within them.

So when we can see God's spirit within people, what that means is, *"I see myself in them, and they in me, and I realize we are of One Heart, that their suffering is my suffering, their joy is my joy."* And when we think this way, how can't we love everyone?

By God's Grace

So, in summation, this is how I experienced my Salvation and resurrection in the Spirit. Or, if you are a follower of Eastern philosophy, how I experienced *samadhi* or attained Realization of the Atman by sacrificing the ego. It is all one and the same.

In the beginning, you can see how an existential crisis led to the dissolution of the ego, which led to my complete and utter absolution by the grace of God.

I did nothing to merit this knowledge; it was gifted to me by God's grace; I am not above anyone; I deserve no acknowledgment; I desire no praise; I only wish to serve and to give; only God is Perfect, so all glory goes to Him.

I deeply want everyone to have this vision, to know God within themselves, to see how we all share the same Self, the same Spirit. I feel like it would solve every problem and alleviate every suffering. But how can I give this knowledge to a single soul, if I can't love them first as God loves them? *And so by that, we must always love first.*

You cannot teach spiritual knowledge without imparting perfect love, *for it is Love that teaches.*

I am simply a mirror reflecting back on you the knowledge you know within yourself. And the highest knowledge is Divine Love, and Divine Love is Unity.

My concept of God to this day comes from this pure experience and His holy companionship within my heart. So when I share insights or commentaries or thoughts, I draw much of my inspiration from this experience, which remains with me as though it happened only five minutes ago. It is important to understand that this knowledge does not fade, because God's name is *"I Am."* I Am is within the body—it is part of you—and after resurrection and receiving God's Light, we cannot go back, for there is simply nothing to return to. Apart from God, *I do not exist*. To erase this experience from my life would be to erase myself from existence. It is, in fact, not simply the day of my rebirth, *but the day of my true birth*. Before this day, I did not exist. I do not know the girl who died, but she is not the one I am now.

Those who have experienced God's Love in this way know exactly what I mean.

A Universal Experience and a Knowledge Deeply Human

Although I have been granted much by the grace of God, I still study and try to defer to the great spiritual masters of the past, because for something to be True, it should be confirmed by multiple sources. I consider myself an eternal student.

Do not take my word on anything; I want you to think for yourself and riddle it out yourself. I have been handed a ring of keys and I was told to give them to you, but take nothing at face value. Try the key in every door, test everything I say, hone your discernment, pray always for guidance and listen to your heart of hearts. You will find the Truth therein.

Ultimately, *you are the path,* it is growing in you, guiding you, becoming you, and by this alone shall you ascend, by this alone shall you attain the vision.

The fact that this experience of Liberation, or Enlightenment, or Salvation, is *universal* and witnessed throughout the world, proves that it is real. It is not unique to me, nor does it belong solely to me, nor am I the gatekeeper to it. Anyone can know God this way, if you seek with all your heart.

I want you to find Him for yourself. It's not an easy task and there is a lot of misinformation to sift through. So with patience and a bit of grace, please allow me to shine a lantern upon this Hidden Kingdom of the heart, with insights gained from sacred dreams and visions, and bolstered by study and reading. It is difficult to put these high-minded concepts into words, and finding the language to do so is a far greater challenge than one might expect. So in these writings, you might find elements of Sufism, Buddhism, Kabbalah, Christian mysticism and Vedanta all mixed together in harmonious unity, and this is by design.

In this collection specifically, I wish to discuss the nature of this Hidden Kingdom in which we dwell, which lends itself to certain spiritual laws and concepts we can use in our everyday lives, that we might avoid certain pitfalls and increase our joy of living. *I want you to have joy in your life.* Pure joy, every day. And certainty in your own existence, in your purpose, and freedom in God, and knowledge of your inheritance as His Child.

Allow me to illuminate the unity and the profundity of spiritual Truth as experienced across the ages. And by that, my sincere and heartfelt prayer is that you will discover this great and mighty Companion within your heart. I wish for you to attain the vision of God. To experience unity and resurrection within the Spirit. To attain that pure and perfect peace of Being. That alone is my reward.

May God's light become your light. May this flame ignite your flame. May this vision become your vision. Let this treasure not be coveted, but given to the world.

The final freedom lies within your heart. Always turn the lantern back on You.

The Hidden Kingdom
Unveiling the Mysteries of God

We live in a Hidden Kingdom.

Christ taught of this Hidden Kingdom, which He and all the prophets bore witness to.

And indeed, the great teachers across all spiritual traditions within the Tree of Life have witnessed God's hidden majesty through the pure heart.

As described in Part I of this book, and witnessed as well within holy scriptures, God is Spirit.

Spirit is of another realm entirely: Heaven.

Spirit transcends the scope of gender. So in the brief essays and commentaries to come, I at times refer to God as "Father" or "Mother," interchangeably as "He" or "She" or "It." This is not to lessen God, nor to commit any sort of heresy against a particular faith, nor to indicate some distinction between masculine and feminine energies—not at all. Rather, I simply interchange these pronouns to demonstrate that God's Spirit is equally present within both man and woman, and all facets of creation are contained within and transcended by the One.

"The Father" is from the patriarchal tradition of Judaism. My personal faith, though baptized and heavily rooted in Christian tradition, is a bit more barefoot and grassroots. I simply mean to remain authentic by enlivening these ancient truths in the language of the modern day. I think it is time to welcome back "The Mother" to our spiritual lexicon, understanding that the Mother and the Father are One, indistinguishable from each other, just different ways of relating to the same great Spirit of Life.

Through visions, dreams and inspired knowledge, the following essays are unveilings of the nature of this Hidden Kingdom, shared in the humble hope of restoring sight to the blind, and awakening souls to the presence of God within.

Let all that I do and say be in service to the highest Love.

The Tree of Life
A REVELATION OF THE NATURE OF HEAVEN

Very subtle, indeed, is this Hidden Kingdom of God. It cannot be touched, tasted or smelled; it cannot be seen, understood or heard except through the pure heart and the illumined mind.

Yet after this Illumination, miracles, visions and inspired dreams become part of everyday life. What might be termed "psychic experiences" or "superconscious knowledge" is folded within the everyday pattern of daily life: school, work, chores, and paying bills. And in fact, such encounters are so regular, the illumined mind simply accepts them as part of him or herself, without pride or boasting, for all things are seen to proceed from God.

My vision of the Tree of Life has been discussed in two other books: *The Book of the Tree of Life* and *Spiritual: A Memoir*. However, as it is significant to my spiritual calling, I will discuss it here as well. The following I consider more than just a vision, but *a revelation*, as it was a hard event revealing the nature of God and the soul through sacred experience.

This vision of the Tree of Life came upon me suddenly, unprompted, when I was twenty-five years old, during a meditation session that was part of Rapid Resolution Therapy (RRT.) This particular kind of therapy uses techniques such as guided meditation, roleplay, storytelling and other types of communication to address trauma. In this instance, I agreed to RRT therapy as I was grieving the loss of my father to a sudden heart attack.

Here is a brief description of RRT from Wikipedia:

"RRT does not only target the conscious thinking brain, but also addresses the emotional brain and limbic system, changing how the unconscious mind processes information so that improvements are natural and automatic. The unconscious mind does not respond immediately to conscious direction but is known to relate and respond quickly to symbols, metaphors, stories, and imagery, so RRT looks to change the neural pathway through specialized tools and techniques like guided meditation, roleplay, and other types of communication. By working with both the conscious, thinking mind and addressing the deeper part of the unconscious mind, RRT can

eliminate the emotional charge associated with the particular traumatic memory or issue. For treating one issue, the typical RRT process is usually completed within one to three online or in-person meetings."

During my first session of Rapid Resolution Therapy, my therapist (we'll call her "Jenn") asked me to imagine a place that brings me peace and makes me feel at home. I thought of the forests up in Washington, where I lived in my childhood before I moved to Los Angeles when I was 10 years old. I missed the forests fiercely in my heart, and on some days, I could feel my whole body crave the peace of the forest. We agreed that the forest would be my "place of sanctuary" as we explored my traumatic experiences together.

After discussing some aspects of my life and the traumatic events of the past few years, Jenn led me through a guided meditation session.

I was sitting in a chair with my feet both on the ground. We faced each other.

She asked me: "Do you believe that we are all connected?"

I said, "Yes."

She took my hand and led me down into a folded position. I bowed my head low, *low* until it was almost between my knees, and I wrapped my arms around myself to calm my nervous system. She released my hand, then she held her hands over the base of my skull.

I breathed deeply, settling into the moment.

"Go to your forest, where you feel safe. I want you to picture the forest and relax. Be at peace."

I breathed deeply and slowly, and in my mind, I went to sit at the base of a peaceful pine tree deep in the forest. I was somewhere in Washington State. Dry pine needles cushioned me. I could smell the scent of warm summer: sweet blackberry perfume in the air. The scent of pine trees and moist earth. Yellow flowers sprinkled my feet. I leaned back against the trunk of the tree and relaxed. I breathed deeply, steadily. All was silence.

As I relaxed, I slowly began to sink backwards. I sank into the tree, into the ground, until I was comfortably wrapped in the roots of the tree. I felt so safe. The earth was so quiet. In the cool moist darkness of the earth, nothing could reach me, and I could sleep and sleep and restore my soul. I felt a wellspring of peace expand inside of me, pulling me down, down into the roots of the tree. I kept sinking deeper and deeper into silence, into peace.

Then, suddenly, I was standing in a chamber that resided inside the heart of the tree, deep underground at the center of the roots. Inside this chamber, I saw a sarcophagus of white stone. It lay horizontally on its side. A beam of sunlight shone down through the center of the tree, illuminating it. The carving of an ancient King lay on top of the sarcophagus, with a stone sword clutched in his hands and a stone crown upon his head.

Suddenly, my dad's presence became *known*. I can describe it no other way. *I knew this was my dad's grave.* He was not visible, yet I felt him right there next to me in the roots of the tree.

In an instant, the Tree exploded around me, growing and growing, shooting thousands of feet into the air. It became the largest Tree you could fathom, stretching up and up into the Heavens, into infinity, into eternity! I felt my dad's spirit join with my own. Our spirits became One, and we took off and flew up through the center of the Tree. *Up and up!* Then the indescribable unity of the Presence of God enveloped us. This immense spirit, emanating from within, embraced us on all sides, and God became One with us.

As One Soul, We flew up through the Tree, becoming One with the Tree itself. And I Knew this:

My dad, myself, God, and the Tree were all ONE.

My dad was not dead. No one was dead. No one ever dies. We were all alive, and we were all together, and we were all growing into a massive Tree, and the Tree was God, and the Tree was infinite, eternal, and contained All Things.

God showed me the Tree of Life.

He showed me the Truth of Life.

There is no death, only life, only a million million lives all growing into One Tree—One God.

God is the Tree of Life, and the Tree contains All Things.

I came out of the vision with tears streaming from my eyes, crying and laughing as grief poured out of my heart. My brain was electric. A great Love and Presence embraced me. I cried with Jenn and hugged her, and in the grief was joy, because I knew my dad's presence again. Somehow, I had reconnected with him *internally*, and I could still feel him with me, inside of my heart. My anxiety was gone, and I felt a renewed sense of peace. I knew now, with a *knowing* beyond knowing, that our spirits were not separate, but One; that we were all One; that my father was not lost, but part of me, part of God, and we were all growing as One eternal Tree of Life.

Heaven is Always Listening

Through this vision, God showed me how all souls are One. The journey of the soul begins and ends with unification with God, and so this is what it means to enter Heaven: to find union with Him.

I became one with my father's spirit, then One with the Father's Spirit. This vision-experience was possible through the purified heart, which I received when I was a child by His grace. I do not think these insights come by any other means but through God's spiritual illumination of our consciousness.

Yet, purehearted or not, all of us are connected by this shared spirit of higher Love, which we can call the Tree of Life.

So here is another secret of the Hidden Kingdom: **our souls are all connected as One, and therefore, Heaven is always listening.**

Knowing that Heaven is a state of pureheartedness, in which we experience this oneness of Spirit, just think of how many people throughout the history of human civilization have entered into this state of unity. All of the saints, apostles, prophets, gurus, siddhas, buddhas, and jivamukti are all One with us, our consciousness shared through the Tree of Life, *and so they are always listening*. This state does not end after we die but continues *into eternity*. They are still alive and listening to our heartfelt pleas and prayers because these higher realms of existence are *purehearted*. We might not be aware of them, but they are aware of us through the Tree of Life. They hear us with a love beyond judgment. They send us help and aid. *They descend to live among us to illuminate the world.*

Often, the voice that speaks from within us, which we attribute to the Holy Spirit or the Higher Self, is *Their voice*. It lends itself to peace, tranquility, wisdom, and insight. Their guidance serves to untie our inner knots and free us from bondage.

So then, through this vision, we can see that God revealed more than just the nature of the Tree of Life but the Godhead itself: infinite souls all growing into One massive Tree of Eternity. Once we receive purification of the heart, we enter into the Tree of Life. Then God's knowledge becomes our knowledge. God's ways become our ways. God lives through us, as much as we live in God. And this unity with the Godhead or "divine Consciousness" is the Heaven and the Kingdom experienced by Christ. It is immanent . . . and it is inside of you, too.

We are all One in the Tree of Life.

For that reason, although I serve God and I am very happy to say I serve Christ, I cannot say, "I do not serve the Buddha." Nor can I say, "I do not serve Ramakrishna," nor can I say, "I do not serve the Tao." To serve One is to serve All in the Tree of Life, and to call myself a servant of One is to call myself a servant of All.

Therefore, I cannot love one religion and hate another. This is against Heaven's will.

I cannot love one believer but hate another. This is against Heaven's will.

Our diversity is designated—it is part of the world. It is not to be annihilated or hated. It *must* be embraced with Love. God's Kingdom lies within the pure heart, within the experience of love and unity with all life, and this is the only path to peace.

It is our blindness and ignorance that lends itself to division, tribalism and hatred. A truly illuminated mind understands every Way, and sees them all as roots to the same Tree: pathways carved through the wilderness of the earth to draw souls into the Garden of Heaven.

In this Work, we truly shine.

The Fireflies and the Lantern

THE BODY OF GOD

The following vision came to me in the most mundane way when I was thirty-four years old, about a year before the writing of this book. I was attending the Vedanta Society of Seattle, a spiritual center run by monks that teaches Eastern philosophy. The Vedanta Society believes in "unity in diversity" and the harmony of all religions. One of the oldest texts in Hinduism, the Rig Veda, states in simple terms: *"Truth is one, sages call it by various names."*

During this time in my life (my early 30's,) God had placed a strong call in my heart to learn to meditate. My husband recommended the Vedanta Society of Seattle because it was nearby, where I met Swami Satyamayananda, the president of their small community. He was the first person to validate my childhood experience of God as not only being *possible* but also well-studied. He taught me about Self-Realization. Although I never became an official devotee of the center *(I had already given my will to*

God, and felt that I could not do so twice,) I learned to meditate under Satyamayananda's guidance. I had many mystical experiences while attending the center, where I received certain spiritual activations that allowed me to see energy bodies. My attainment of certain siddhas was largely due to being helped by Sri Ramakrishna—who still visits me often in dreams, assists with energy cultivation and showers me in gifts.

For those who are curious, during my first dream of Sri Ramakrishna, I found myself in a temple deep in the jungle. This temple was a school of sorts, a spiritual academy full of orange-robed monks. The temple was built of plain stone with no adornments. The buildings were shaped like step pyramids, and the stones had a brownish-golden hue with a distinct feeling of age. I saw many different pyramid-shaped buildings, courtyards and cloistered walkways. I spent the majority of the dream chasing after Sri Ramakrishna, who was teaching at the center. I felt like we were playing "hide and seek." Whenever I saw him, he was walking somewhere far off, always surrounded by a crowd of monks. I would traverse the many walkways and staircases to try to reach the pavilion where I had seen him, but it seemed like whenever I reached the area, he would be gone. Then I would glimpse him again walking somewhere far off, and I would chase after him.

By the end of the dream, I had lost track of him and decided to give up. I was standing in a covered walkway between one of the temples and an open pavilion surrounded by palm and fig trees. Then, suddenly, Ramakrishna was before me. His eyes were shining very brightly. I had a very clear sense of his presence. He smiled at me and took hold of my arms, his hands clasping me elbow-to-elbow as he gazed deep into my eyes. *Then dark blue fire flared up around him, like an aura, and we were both engulfed in indigo fire.* We burned together in the blue fire. Then the dream ended.

After that, Ramakrishna would often find me in my dreams, and I have returned to this forest school many times.

For those who have read my memoir, these sorts of mystical experience have followed me all of my life, so although my encounters with Ramakrishna were frequent, I didn't think anything of them at the time. As I was new to Vedanta, I didn't know the significance of the blue fire. Several months passed before I described the dream to Swami Satyamayananda, who explained to me the connection between the blue fire and Mother Kali.

For the sake of inclusion, I say this for the benefit of those who are Hindu or who practice Vedanta: God wears many faces, and Ramakrishna is one of my teachers. We, too, are connected in the Tree of Life. As for the divine Mother—there is only one Light. The Mother and the Father are One.

The Vision of the Lantern

During this time, I was experiencing a period of "spiritual revival" after leaving my job, retreating from the world and spending time in meditation and prayer. By grace, I received a purification experience that restored my mind for this Work. And this is when I experienced the most mundane vision of the Lantern.

One afternoon, I was sitting on my couch in the living room watching TV.

I saw an image flash across the TV screen: a glowing lantern at night surrounded by a cloud of bobbing, dancing fireflies *(not unlike the cover of this book.)*

I felt *a strong nudge*. I heard God's voice say through my heart, *"That's Me."*

Now, God's voice is unmistakable when you hear it. God is not wordy or verbose. It is not like hearing a human voice at all. The Spirit imparts direct knowledge internally with only a few short words, which comes through our consciousness very sudden, very clear. Those words are imbued with layers of meaning several oceans deep. Like seeds planted in the earth, it can take time for the full meaning to sprout and grow and overtake our conscious mind. But not so in this case. In this case, I heard the words clearly and their meaning was immediate.

(*Sometimes God uses an image instead of a word, just a flash of an image through the mind, yet the image is imbued with an essay's worth of meaning and immediate comprehension. God also communicates this way through dreams.*)

With those two words—*"That's Me"*—I was struck by the understanding that I was gazing at the body of God. *We are the fireflies, and He is the Lantern.* My eyes were drawn to the light throughout the lantern, which seemed to envelope the fireflies like an ocean and hold them suspended in an ambient glow, even as they danced and bobbed around, each one lit from within.

Then the remembering—*oh yes*—the multiplicity and the unity—the fireflies within the Lantern—and all the same Light.

And from that vision came the following essay on the structure of Consciousness, also known as "the body of God."

Imagine an old-world lantern, the kind that has a flame inside of it. And this lantern is filled by a warm, ambient glow. A beautiful white flame glows at the center of the lantern, and then a warm, soft light pervades throughout.

And within this lantern are fireflies.

The fireflies are all bobbing about, darting and spinning around as fireflies do.

We see, however, the Light within the firefly and the Light within the lantern are One. They are the same Light.

And so by imagining this, we can start to understand the body of God, or how we can visualize God in this three-dimensional world.

God is the Lantern, and we are the fireflies.

We are inside the Lantern, and the Lantern is also inside of us.

Just as the lantern is lit and pervaded with light, so we, too, the individual fireflies, are lit and pervaded with light.

The light of the firefly and the light of the Lantern are One.

They are the same Light.

A Quest for Illumination

As you look at these fireflies, you will see that certain ones are a little more dim, and certain ones are a little bit more bright. And every now and then, one of these fireflies bursts and ignites, and realizes itself as sharing the same light as the Lantern.

Then this little firefly can look around and see that this same Light is within all of the other little fireflies, too.

From that moment on, the firefly no longer identifies as "just" a firefly, but as One with the Lantern.

A tiny lantern within a larger Lantern.

And then it goes about the Work of igniting the other fireflies, getting them to shine a little brighter, getting them to think a little more about their own light within, trying to demonstrate the light of the lantern:

"Look at this glow, look at this beautiful Light that we dwell within!

It is the same light that dwells within us."

The Body of God

So when contemplating the body of God, what we can understand is that we are inside of God, and God is inside of us.

In the sense that we are God's children, God is at once both the Lantern and the firefly, and yet the fireflies are not always aware that they are the Lantern. As children, our perspective is limited.

And as long as we identify as "just" a firefly, we are only existing in part. We are not fully aware of our own existence, and we're not fully aware of *what we are*, because we do not know our own Light.

We have not yet become *"Self-illuminated."*

And yet, when that light ignites within, we see it is the same light as the whole Lantern, and then we desire nothing more than to ignite the Light in others.

And so I wish to encourage you, little firefly, to remember that the Light within you is the same Light in others, and that the Light within your heart is the very Light of God, and you are One with all of this existence.

The Qualities of the Lantern

When perceiving the Lantern through our spiritual eyes, we see the pure spirit of God pervading all matter, similar to an ocean or a cloud, but it does not have substance in the sense that an ocean or a cloud has substance. It is more of a vibration.

And just like one long, unbroken note, a Perfect C sustained into eternity, this vibration has no gap to it, no variation, no coming or going, no rising or falling, no distortion. This great Note is eternal, unchanging, endless, pure, without beginning or end: *I AM.*

This is the root of all Being. It is God. It is Self.

So in an ocean, we have waves: each wave is choppy and maybe a little bit bigger or a little bit smaller than the next wave, but it's all the same water. No one questions that the substance of the wave and the substance of the ocean is the same.

Likewise, within the Lantern, we see each firefly is a bit different than the next, some glowing brighter, some dimmer, yet we should not question it is all the same Light.

Therefore, when we perceive the body of God, although on the surface it might look like many waves or many patterns or bubbles of light, what we are perceiving is just One. God's Light is undifferentiated from Itself. There isn't anything that's more God or less God in this universe. It's all just One. And that is the vibration, "I AM." That's God's name. The pure Note.

So this Presence is a *resonance*. It's not substance, it's more essence or vibration, like what you would hear if you were in a concert hall and there was a great symphony going on. The music is filling up all of the rafters and the walls and your ears and your mind and your heart. The outside and the inside are One Song. It's a sense of music that is so powerful, it becomes a Presence and a Will within and throughout everything.

There is a light to it. It is not the kind of light we see with our eyes, that would be a heavy light, almost like a dirty light, due to its effect on the material world. The Lantern is pure, it is the light of the Spirit, it is untouched and unaffected by gross or subtle matter, it shines within you and it shines without. Its Source is everything. It is everywhere. And it's rooted in your heart. It is within you. And so you can know this Light as the root of yourself. It is its own Source.

And that's the Lantern.

It is living.

It is fully sentient, *more so than the fireflies*. It is omniscient and omnipresent. In Her eyes, we are but little bubbles of light or little fireflies darting about, sustained by Her body, and She watches us play.

We like to think of this holy Light as a "power" or an "energy" with no intelligence or self-awareness. We think of "Consciousness" as a static, sterile concept in a philosophy book. *But the Lantern is Living.* It is Life itself. It is far more Self-aware than any man or woman. In fact, compared to Her awareness, we exist as shadows. And so that is why we call Her Mother or Father, because She is infinitely higher than us, to be revered and exalted, and that is how She wishes to be known.

It can be hard to comprehend. It is truly beyond the unillumined mind.

Just know that She belongs to you, and you belong to Her.

The Qualities of the Fireflies

Now let's consider the fireflies.

Within this lantern are many fireflies. The fireflies are of the pure Light, but as long as they think of themselves as fireflies, they don't know their own purity. And the fireflies are like bubbles floating around inside of this larger Lantern. And within those bubbles, we see the same Light contained at the heart of each one that pervades the whole Lantern. And this Light sustains the firefly; it gives it breath and being; likewise, it holds all of the laws of the universe in place, and keeps the cosmos dancing to a great harmony.

The fireflies don't know themselves to be within a Lantern. They don't know the source of their own Light. Their knowledge is incomplete, and so their existence is only partially experienced, because they are bobbing around in relative darkness, and they have not yet discovered the Light within.

And so we see subtle variations between the different fireflies, like a cloud obscuring their purity. Every firefly is capable of realizing the Lantern, but some fireflies have dimmed themselves. Others shine a little brighter. And this correlates to our spiritual body and our relative faith. In the spiritual body, the more love and faith you have, the brighter the firefly shines, until it realizes the Lantern.

Loving kindness, faith, virtue—cultivating these traits opens the heart to the divine and purifies the spirit.

Now, there are some fireflies who are very dark and run about like little bees. They go from dark to dark, from life to life, and without some intervention, never spare a thought for the Lantern or the other fireflies.

Other fireflies move from dark to light. They first appear dim, but as they seek after their own light, they become more and more agitated. And then, in a burst of willpower, they suddenly ignite and realize the Lantern. They explode from darkness to light, a sort of kamikaze firefly, and this can happen.

And yet more fireflies have some idea that the Lantern exists, and so they conscientiously, step-by-step, increase their faith by measure and discover the Lantern this way. And so their Light increases by measure as they cultivate virtues and proceed with a lengthy, arduous path of growth.

Finally, we see a few fireflies that go from light to light—very old, gracious and loving fireflies—whose simple purpose is to help illuminate the Way. These are very rare indeed, very large and luminous, and they are the most beautiful to watch.

As the true nature of every firefly is the same nature as the Lantern, each firefly will eventually ignite and realize itself as One with the pure Light. It is the fate and the destiny of every firefly to become the Lantern. The only question is *when.*

When the firefly discovers the Light within itself, becoming "resurrected" or Self-illuminated, it realizes its own body as One with the Lantern and therefore, also One with the cloud of fireflies around it. All things are seen to be One.

Then the firefly discovers its sacred duty.

The Self-illuminated firefly no longer has any desire for itself, as it sees itself existing as One with the whole Lantern. So this little firefly's sacred duty, and truest desire, is to increase the light of the whole Lantern by illuminating others, so that every firefly might know its true nature.

How can a Firefly Illuminate Others?

In order to awaken her brethren, this Self-illuminated little firefly is given gifts through which the Lantern might increase its glow. These gifts are meant to stir the heart and awaken the spirit of others.

The pure flame, now contained within the Self-illuminated firefly, can be passed to other fireflies through Prayer, Creativity, Presence, and Word.

These are just artful expressions of the pure Light within.

What is created with purity stimulates purity in others. It is a chain reaction.

And so this is how the pure firefly goes about its Work, as both the firefly and the Lantern.

- It creates beautiful music, poetry and art to stimulate a sense of holiness and divinity within others, reminding us of the dignity of our own souls.
- It speaks beautiful sermons to inspire worship and devotion to God and to higher ideals, that we might live in righteousness and virtue.
- Through a reverent or loving touch, embrace or laughter, She passes Her purity through her loving presence.

- Through prayer, She awakens the hearts of others by stimulating their awareness internally, moving behind walls, moving others through the unified Will.

- She does not boast, speak ill of other fireflies (even when they are behaving as bumblebees), judge, curry favor or play favorites. She loves and embraces all the fireflies equally, for she knows at heart She is the Lantern.

- With great love, She moves the world by opening the hearts of others.

- She dwells within the pure heart, honoring the truest desire of Her soul: to be Good, and do this Good Work.

- She fears not the fiery tongues of men, knowing She is the Lantern, inextinguishable, residing within the heart of all life.

- In courage, She perseveres ever toward Her goal of bringing Light to other fireflies and to the world.

This pure firefly dedicates her life to the illumination of others, seeking to encourage and inspire others in faith, by helping others find the Light within.

The Mother and the World
A MYSTICAL DREAM

Not very long ago in her life, this whimsical author had a beautiful dream. Within this dream, she knew herself to be the Mother of All, and she stood, her body spread throughout the cosmos, surrounded by stars and glowing galaxies, to gaze down upon the blue orb of the Earth.

She felt herself to be in a creative mood. With great care and attention, she reached down and began plucking paint brushes off the surface of the Earth, each one a unique color and length from the last, inspecting and studying each paint brush with tenderness, trying to select the perfect one for her Work. For you see, the Earth was Her canvas, and the Universe was Her workshop. And each paint brush She plucked from the ground to examine was a person, a man or a woman utterly unique in their gifts and qualities, and She was choosing which one She would work through, to create Her grand and beautiful design.

She had a painting in mind, you see, and She was enjoying herself, placing the brush to the canvas.

Upon waking, this whimsical woman knew herself to be simply a paint brush in the hands of a great Artist—an expression of Creativity of a Life much greater than her own—and she saw that all of the world and all of the Universe was, indeed, a work of sacred Art by the hands of a very great Mother.

Sunlight

Find me, God, and chase me into Sunlight—
bloom me 'neath the moon and show me
what is midnight, and what is the darkness
that we keep within ourselves.

I know your textures, your colors and sounds
and wherever I walk, it is your call that resounds
in the air, like an echo—I see through an ocean
of open wonder, your Presence profound

in the wind that I breathe, and the walls where I rest;
I feel you in the ground, in the grass at my feet
and the asphalt trees, the sky blooming heat
with the weight of your thoughts like a fire in me!

So chase me! Remember, we met as children, alone,
and now a woman awakens within my breast—
oh dear, sweet Lover, drag me without
and thrust me in Daylight, explain me the ways

you've laid at my feet, the truths in my chest
and the words in my lungs that strain to be said—
yes, it all makes sense like nothing makes sense—
this Love in the deepest chambers of me!

And if you doubt me, friend, let my presence prove
that this Love within me shall be given to you.
Study my heart, dissect me with care,

but I am standing in Sunlight, and there is Sunlight to
share.

In the Heart of Man

I live and dwell
in the heart of man,

yet who,

pray tell,

shall dwell within Me?

Some call me eternal,

a gateway of light,

you've met me,

you've held me,

yet none know my plight.

Some call me Nirvana,

a doorway to God,

yet I am in nature,

in life,

I am Love.

I live and dwell

in a silent oasis,

in a world of no faces

the most secluded of places.

You'll find me waiting

in the pause between raindrops,

the space between heartbeats,

that place where your heart stops.

I find my reason

between dreaming and waking,

between forgiving and praying,

between giving and taking--
I find the reason,
the reason for saying
that I--
I am Love.
And I dwell in the heart of man.

White

I reached
to feel all of the things
You changed inside of me.

Yet still
my hands probe the soft tissues
and find only white,
white as silence,
white as the needle
injected in my spine,
white as the current of power
upshot like a bullet to the clouds
before lightning strikes the earth.

Whiter than the surface of a star.

I can place one hand
where the white begins,
and one hand where it ends,
and yet somehow
by the laws of numbers
I know it proceeds inward *inward*
endlessly,
melting deeper and deeper
until the center is relative;
until infinity is the only answer.

And my fingers seek to feel all
that's new inside of me,
knowing You've become my soul.

"This Moment"

Let this moment be a memory,
    To be perfect,
    Be divine,
    Frozen in an instant
    To resist the rust of time.

Let this moment be a portrait,

Something gorgeous,

Something pure,

Let this moment be the moment

That will always be endeared.

Let this minute last a lifetime,

In the silence,

In the dark,

Let these words create a shelter

That will never fall apart;

Let this minute be forever,

Be eternal,

Be my dream,

Let this minute show me everything

My eyes have never seen.

Let this second be a cycle,

A renewal,

A rebirth.

Let this second be the moment

That we change the course of Earth,

Let this second be my destiny,

My infinity,

My soul . . .

Let this second teach me everything

I'll ever need to know.

The Giver of Gifts
GOD IS A MULTIPLIER

Agarden can teach us wonderful things about this Hidden Kingdom, if we can be quiet for a moment and observe.

My husband loves sunflowers and popcorn. So this past Spring, we planted a bunch of sunflowers and a lot of corn.

And I remember specifically planting the sunflowers across the yard with a little stick and making holes about one inch deep, and putting a sunflower seed in every single hole. And by the end of June, six-foot tall sunflowers were beginning to sprout up out of the ground. Then by the end of August, the sunflowers were eleven feet tall, and their heads were bigger than dinner plates! They were full of sunflower seeds. *(We planted the Mammoth variety.)*

And so, for each sunflower seed that we put in the ground, up came at least a hundred more seeds per flower.

From twenty seeds came two thousand.

We also planted corn this last spring. We planted about ten rows and five columns, so one-hundred-and-fifty little seeds went into the ground. And if you've ever grown your own corn, then you know where this is going. From a mere handful of seeds, we got back nine pounds of popcorn.

Not nine handfuls, not nine cups, *nine pounds.*

And by this very attribute of nature, we can catch a glimpse of this hidden, spiritual Kingdom in which we dwell.

God is a Multiplier

Once the eyes of the heart are illuminated, by observing the workings of nature, we can understand the character of this magnanimous Spirit of Life that resides within the world, that exists around us at all times.

One seed becomes one thousand.
So, we can see that God is a multiplier.
God is the "Giver of Gifts."
God is the One who has become the Many,
and so God takes One and creates Many.
It is what God does.

This great Spirit needs nothing from us. You've probably heard this before, but God is doing everything, *everything,* all of the time, and so we don't need to do anything by ourselves. We should simply busy ourselves with learning God's ways, pray often, and trust this great Mother of Life to guide us through every trial into peace.

These gifts that She gives are just what She is.
Because Her nature is the Giver of Gifts.

And this multiplying is happening in every corner of the cosmos, every second of the day, and some astrophysicists estimate somewhere between 200,000 to 1 million stars are being born per minute across the Universe.

So for those of you trying to understand the nature of God and the unseen reality in which we live, this is what the pure Spirit of Life is like. He (or She) is just endless giving.

She is wholeness itself, and this wholeness, this pure and perfect Consciousness residing at the heart of the cosmos, has a nature, and that nature is simple. It gives.

It IS and it GIVES.

Children of a Great Mother

We are Her children.
We are little dandelion seeds of Her soul
floating around in a cosmic wind

She carries us
to our appointed time and place,
and gives us what is good for our soul.

She gives us fertilizer, the Sun,
the water and the nutrients.

Did you know that some seeds
like Hollyhocks or Coneflowers
cannot bloom unless they have
endured several months of frost?

So, She gives us the frost as well.
And because She is all things and sustains all things,
She knows what is best for every soul,
and you can trust Her to give these gifts
to you at the right time, just as every flower
has its own appointed time to bloom.

She gives us what we are, toward the purpose of bringing us into unity and harmony with Her spirit.

Like a leaf dancing on the wind, we cannot comprehend Her pattern nor the path our lives might take, and yet dancing, we come to Her

All things move toward this purpose of unity, because the vision of Her is the greatest gift that can be given, and this union with Her is the Divine will.

Learning to move with Her through the small, mundane yet miraculous moments of our lives, is how we give away the ego and become One with Her.

The Spiritual Practice of Giving

As human beings, we are not very good at giving gifts.
We struggle with this part of our nature.

We always give gifts for specific reasons. When we're little, we want to give a gift to someone because we love them very much. But then maybe, sometimes, it has to be the right gift because we want to please someone and we know they're picky.

Or maybe there's somebody at school who we actually don't like very much, and so we try a little bit less to give them a nice gift, because they're not our favorite person.

And this is how people are. It's how children are, but it's also how adults are, too.

As we get older, we learn to give gifts in an adult way, which usually means we give for an ulterior motive. We're either giving gifts to keep the peace, because it would be rude to forget someone's birthday or to skimp on Christmas. Or we give gifts as an apology; we hurt someone or we fell out of their good graces, and to make it up to them, we buy them something nice or we bring them a coffee at work. Or we give gifts to win favor; maybe we're doing business with a new client or a new customer and we really want to win their business, so they can give us money. So we are giving them gifts with the idea of reciprocity in mind, that we want to strike up a business deal, and this is the language of business. It's not necessarily manipulation, but there is an aspect of manipulation to it, because you're trying to win favor for an ulterior motive, not just for love and the desire to give.

We are very imperfect in the body, and this is one of the ways we can tell how far we fall from God's perfect Love. Because this great Spirit of Life gives gifts for the sake of giving. She needs nothing from anyone, and there is no one for Her to curry favor with. She loves all equally. And we all belong to Her. So Her gifts are genuine, magnanimous, endless, and without condition. They're unconditional gifts. And they're given for no reason. Except maybe that we might allow Her to multiply them through us. And we can see this when a musician becomes a teacher and gives the gift of music to twenty, thirty, sometimes forty children per classroom, per semester, year after year after year.

This is simply another example of God multiplying Her gifts.

The Gift of Perfect Love

So when Christ says we should strive to be perfect as our Father is in Heaven, this is a small window into what He means.

We should give gifts for the sake of giving.
Because giving itself is joy.
And we should accept gifts
only if they are given freely
in the spirit of joy.
And in fact, the material aspect
of a gift isn't truly real.
In this secret, hidden Spiritual Kingdom,
what we are giving is the Joy itself,
and that is the same as giving Life.
And if we can let that Joy of Giving
penetrate the heart and reside within us,
then we can take it into a hundred thousand
lifetimes to come,
and   it   becomes   what   we   are.

Long ago, when I wrote my first spiritual essay, even though it was only a few pages long, I felt exhausted. This Work takes all of my soul to do. As I walked through my house, I felt the Spirit move in my heart. In a gentle way, that soft inner voice said, "Sit down. Be in Me. I have words for you."

As I sat down and went inward to be in that oasis of peace in the Heart, I felt the Lord say, "Thank you for the gifts." And with profound understanding, I saw what I was doing through God's eyes: I was not writing essays and I was not "working." I was giving. I was giving gifts.

And He showed me how even three words said in Truth shall grow and multiply 100,000 times over. Because He is Truth itself. I understood these teachings were not for me, but they were for Him, gifts given to Him in sincere gratitude for this Salvation. And what I give to God, He will carry like seeds on the wind to fertile soil to set down roots and multiply.

No single act of kindness is ever wasted.

Every word said with sincerity and love makes Life grow.

The Giving of Life

*And so with this understanding, little firefly, realize
that the Work we do is actually the giving of Life.*

That is what He Is.

*So although we might say that Christ is a giver of
gifts, or Krishna or the Buddha is the giver of gifts,
really it is this universal Father or Mother, this
beautiful Tree of Life, who is the Giver of all gifts. For*

the Tree of Life grows on and on, it has no end and no beginning, no one can fathom its size, and yet it grows and grows and grows into Infinity. And as it grows, it gives.

And just like a single sunflower seed
planted in the ground
turns into a thousand more,
so every awakened soul
is a seed planted upon the Earth
to awaken a hundred thousand more.
From One comes Many.
This is the Spirit's play.
She is growing a garden.
A garden made of souls.
And every seed that takes root
gives way to more life, greater life, deeper life,
in this Tree of Life that goes
on and on and on.

There is this idea in Hindu cosmology that Mother Kali, at the end of one cycle of Creation, collects all of the seeds for Her next cycle of Creation. And she is doing this now. Every liberated soul is a seed placed in her pouch that she has collected. She brings us back to Herself, and She keeps us inside of Her heart *preparing for the next Creation. And She will not stop until every seed is gathered. So don't worry, your time will come. That is Mother's promise, it is Her gift, and She is the Giver of Gifts. It is what She does. It is Her will. It is Her way. She will give freely when it is time to give, and our only job is to faithfully follow Her ways and allow Her to bestow the gift upon us.*

So in the same light, strive
to see everything in your life
as given to you by this great Love,
this One: the Giver of All Gifts.
Strive to see the gift in your story,
in each experience.
Remember, everything in this life,
whether we understand it or not,
has been given in the spirit of magnanimous Love.
There is a gift hidden inside of
every aspect of your life.
Learn to see the gift.
Or better yet, ask God to reveal the gift to you,
and see how the heart changes,
how Truth springs up from within.

Remember that you are a gift. You are a gift to your mother. You are a gift to your father. You're a gift to your friends. You are a gift to your employer and your coworkers. You are a gift to your spouse or your lover. You are a gift to your children. You're a gift from God to God.

Remember, not only is there a gift within every trial in your life, but that you too are a flower blooming in this Garden. You carry the seed of eternity within you. You have a place in this cosmic plan, because you are here today with me. So believe in yourself. Because I do.

And if it feels like we cannot make sense of our lives, just speak out and say, "Mother, show me the gift!"

Then Her understanding will come.

The Garden of Souls
THE OPENING OF THE PURE HEART

Little Rose, did you know
that God grows as you grow
and love holds you in sunlight
and shelters you close
as a heart to a soul?

Little Rose, listen close
for God all already knows
when you'll bloom
and your colors: bright, bold, or serene.
He has seen all your seasons
from darkness to dreams.

He planted your seed
and He waters your roots.
As you grow, little soul,
know that God grows in you.

Sometimes, God shows us the soul as a firefly. Sometimes, God shows us the soul as a towering Tree. Sometimes, God shows us the soul as a flower.

And the symbol of Enlightenment is the thousand-petaled lotus.

We hear from different spiritual traditions that Heaven is a garden of sorts, and we already know that the earth is a beautiful place.

If we look around the natural world, we can easily imagine that this Universe is a beautiful, even Divine, garden.

And yet we don't often think of the internal garden of the Heart: the Garden that is inside of us.

In spiritual practice, we should remember that the true Garden is within your heart, and you're growing that day by day

Nature is a Sacred Place

Sometimes we place a shrine in the garden, and yet, the garden itself is sacred.

There is nothing that human hands can do that can make a sacred place more sacred.

This is because God dwells in the garden, just as we do.

And so, although we sometimes go to a church, shrine or a temple to worship God, there is no real need for that. The worship of God is happening everywhere, everywhere, all at once, in this beautiful dance of the cosmos.

The same Spirit of Life that enlivens your own body is also enlivening all of the plants, the insects, and all of the creatures.

There is only one Spirit of Life.

And as they say in some traditions, "Even a rock is a thing pervaded by divinity." (Kabbalah)

Entering the Garden

To find the Garden, we have no farther to look than inside of ourselves. For the garden truly is a heaven that dwells within you, and the gate to that garden is within the heart, and the more we cultivate love of God, the deeper we come into the garden, so that we might find our presence with Him . . . or with Her.

The body truly is the temple, and You are the shrine.

And though we might place crosses around our neck or tattoo a lotus on our arm, there is nothing that human hands can do that can make a sacred place more sacred.

And I want you, Little Rose, to remember that you are the sacred ground, you are the Garden.

As you grow in faith, in life, and within the body, so God is growing within you.

And we can see that growth as we deepen our capacity to love, both ourselves and others, in that gentle, magnanimous, and selfless way.

Lessons from the Garden

Truly, it is a garden of peace, a garden of serenity, a place of quietude and stillness within the heart.

Truly, God's garden grows from within us, just as all things grow from within.

So, as we look about God's garden, we might understand every soul is a flower residing within God's heart, for we are all growing within Him.

And He looks upon each of us as a perfect flower, with no flaw and no imperfection, seeing only His own light within.

So it does not serve us to compare ourselves to others, for everyone comes to the Garden to do their own work in their own unique way.

That is God's gift to them, and that is our gift to God.

We're really not all meant to be great lilies and roses and dahlias and sunflowers, so shocking and eye-catching. Some of us are wildflowers. Some of us are violets.

Just as every flower embodies its own particular type of beauty, so every soul embodies the beauty of God.

So whoever you are, whatever you do, do it with complete contentment, knowing that you do it for God.

Just as God is always here with us, walking through the Garden and tending it with very great care, so we should come to value every person, seeing that every kind of person is needed, and honoring the Light within.

And just as we understand our faith is a seed, so we should understand our soul is a seed growing into God.

The Opening of the Flower

Create in me a pure heart, O God. Renew a right spirit within me.
Psalm 51:10

As we gaze upon this garden, we can see how each of the flowers are a little more open, and some are a little more closed, and this corresponds to the nature of the pure heart.

The flower of the pure heart is fully open and glows white. No trial, grief, depression or loss may close it, no sin may come between the pure heart and Her God.

And yet, many other flowers exist who have turned their faces toward the Sun to receive the holy Light. They glow brightly and their colors are varied and luminous.

Yet other flowers remain closed in dormancy, having yet to bloom, awaiting the Light.

And so by this, we know the quality of the heart by its openness—its receptiveness to God's Love—its cheerfulness, its inner peace, its loving kindness and charity to others.

Still other flowers remain in their infancy, as seeds beginning to sprout. These hearts are yet closed. As seedlings, they work their way up through the darkness of the earth, blind to their own beauty or the beauty in others.

When trial comes upon the open heart, it responds with virtue and great forbearance, and it grows stronger in its faith.

When trial comes upon the closed heart, it closes further, crushed under the weight of its suffering.

And so we see the greatest challenge in life is to endure all things with an open heart.

To resist the darkening, the bitterness, the numbing that comes from emotional loss, the deadening of the spirit, and continually turn toward God or Spirit to help purify the heart, and keep it open to His grace.

Certain gifts have been given to us: Faith, gratitude, friendship, compassion, tranquility, courage and wisdom to endure the trials of life.

Faith is a very great gift, and yet not accessible to all people, depending on the mode of their suffering.

If we cannot have faith, then we can have gratitude.

If we cannot have faith, then we can have compassion, tranquility, courage and wisdom.

Yet truly, a flower's faith allows God's Light to resurrect the soul.

Without faith, there can be no healing.

The River to the Ocean
THE JOURNEY OF THE SOUL

How deep is the soul who loves like the river.
  Little streams of light flow pleasantly
  through to embrace you.
  Never in haste or in vain,
  always a place to remain in the rain.
  Peaceful the words and whimsy the ways,
  meandering under the moon or by day.
  Home is the soul who loves like a river,
  guiding the world toward the ocean.

The Art of Acceptance

If you consider the river, it is always moving.

And yet the river is guided by the banks.

Although the river is moving, in many ways, it is patient.

As it carves its path through the earth, through adversity and *hardness*—eventually that river's purpose is to meet the ocean.

And if we think of a river moving toward the ocean,
it is always persistent,
and yet it moves in its own time.

There are various factors, such as seasons and weather, that impact the river's flow, whether it is fast or slow.

So in this context, we can think of our lives as a great moving river toward the ocean.

Through the years of our lives, as we encounter different people, relationships or circumstances—such as disease, caretaking a loved one, joblessness, or homelessness—we can see how the seasons of our lives impact this great and holy *river of our life* on its path toward the ocean.

And so a simple wisdom comes from this: if we trust ourselves as water trusts itself, then we know that all of the currents of the world are pushing us toward this ocean.

And all we really have to do is stay true to our practice or our faith, and continue to allow life to carry us through the necessary trials that we must endure in order to find the ocean.

Tranquility, Flow, Peace

And so the practice of *tranquility* in your life is *a deep one.*

It begins with sort of a simple knowledge, which is to allow things to occur and arise in their own time.

Not to assert our smaller will over the circumstances of life, but to disengage and allow things to be as they are.

To find the gifts inside of those situations and circumstances which allow us to have peace and contentment with our lives the way they are.

And this allows us to maintain a pure and open heart.

The Inner Work of Peacemaking

This doesn't mean that we cease to work.
And this doesn't mean that we cease to improve
or that we stop having goals.
But we allow things to develop as they will.

And we do our very best with the understanding that at the end of the day, a great part of our lives is outside of our control. And all that we can truly control is our mindset and our reaction to these external circumstances.

A lot of times, we cannot flow with life because we are clinging. We cling to these stories and these ideas that we have about how life should be and how life should go.

And these stories are given to us.
They're not born into us.
They're given to us through society and through culture,
through our parents, our raising,
our background, our religion.

And this creates a framework through which we view the world. And we cling to this framework because, quite frankly, without it, we would feel quite lost. And yet life in its magnitude and its awesomeness has a way of disrupting that framework.

Events occur that are not supposed to occur, according to the story that we have written for ourselves.

We find ourselves in unpredictable circumstances and we don't know how to react. There's no template for that. Anyone who has become a parent is faced with this almost every day. As you shelter a young life and guide a young life into the world, I don't think anyone can prepare truly for parenthood. But it is a great lesson to trust in the flow of life, to trust in the greatness of the soul, and to realize that all of these trials and all of these obstacles are really just to help us as we purify the heart, as we learn and gain Wisdom through the seeking of tranquility within our lives and peace within ourselves.

I think there comes a time that we all feel a need to turn away from the everyday problems and dramas and troubles that the world presents us, and there's an endless amount of them in every arena of life.

And we simply wish to be, we simply wish to have peace. And so this is really the goal and what it means to live in flow, is to live in peace, to have peace in your life, to not engage in behaviors or with people that cause unnecessary conflict.

We do grow through conflict, but I believe the lesson at the end of every conflict is truly a letting go, *a forgiving*.

And so from a Christian perspective, you can understand "flow" as a practice of forgiveness.

Forgiving the ones who've wronged you and becoming a peacemaker between people is how we truly grasp the idea of simply flowing with life, removing our judgments, and practicing a higher love.

In Taoism, this idea is similar to *wu wei*. The idea of *wu wei* is a little bit more cerebral in nature. We understand the Tao is a great force that is always moving through the world, and that by practicing this art of inaction, we are able to disengage from worldly obstacles, and truly move in harmony with the Tao, from which comes the attainment of the Tao or Realization.

And that moment is when the river meets the ocean.

The Practice of Peace

And so flow is the practice of peace.
  It is being a peacemaker among people.
  Flow is having inner quiet, addressing our inner state
and being self-accountable for our inner state.

Recognizing those thoughts that tear us down and lead to confrontational behaviors in our lives or negative self-talk, and truly learning to get a grasp over these inner thoughts and these inner states of mind, and create a very clean inner space for ourselves, where we have a certain amount of peace, both with ourselves and with our relationships with people.

And so a part of this flow is meeting everyone where they are at. And of course, we know the world is full of many different kinds of people, and we don't get along with all of them. Some of them we really struggle to see eye to eye.

And yet, acknowledging that the Divine dwells within every person is an easier way to begin to accept every person as they are, to see everyone as being on their unique journey to God, and perhaps there was a meaning in your encountering them.

And even if there is very little to be gained by that encounter on your side, perhaps the gain was theirs.

Letting Go of Judgments

There is a feeling many of us carry with us, which is a deep-seated feeling of shame. "Shame" is a sense that there is something wrong with the way we are doing things, and we are afraid of being *judged*.

To make peace with our hidden shame, consider that judgment is inescapable. *Everyone* judges. A part of our spiritual practice is to disentangle ourselves from our own judgments toward other people, and that's all we can control.

We cannot control how people perceive us. And you will hear all sorts of strange things that people think about you.

But realize no one ever really sees you.
No one can really know your heart, except God.
And no one can really know your reasons, except God.

And so accept their judgment with a grain of salt.
Forgive it, realizing that no one is perfect.
And if we can come to expect this behavior from people,
it is much easier to forgive it.
Because holding people to a standard higher than where they are at means we are loving conditionally rather than unconditionally.
And every person has a place in the Tree of Life.

Acceptance is a Practice of Love

In summation, the practice of flow is truly a practice of Love.

Loving yourself as you are,
forgiving yourself as you are,
coming to the divine as you are,
learning to love others as they are,
accepting as they are,
seeing them as they are.

And in the same sense,
seeing every obstacle in our life
and every trouble that we are working through
as a divine gift,
that through this struggle,
the river eventually comes to the ocean.

The Song of Being
The Vibration of Consciousness

Close your eyes and see before you the majesty of nature. See a forest of infinite trees spanning into the horizon.

Imagine inside of that forest are shrubs and bushes, ferns and vines and flowers,

rocks and rivers and moss.

Imagine herds of deer, squirrels, rabbits, bobcats and all manner of life

dwelling within that forest.

Each one, uniquely distinct.

And this is the physical world in which we dwell.

Now imagine, for a moment, the forest is not a forest. Imagine the forest as imbued with a subtle, pervasive energy of life. Every tree, every rock, every river, every living thing is subtly vibrating, like a musical instrument, that can be felt and perceived through our spirit. Every object is giving off waves of subtle energy imperceptible to the eye, to the ear, to the skin. It's not radiation, no, it goes deeper than that. It's not heartbeats or the pulse of nature, no, it goes deeper than that.

At the root of every being
is the subtle yet powerful Spirit of Life,
and it is vibrating always
with a great, unitive sound: I AM.

And each of these musical instruments—the trees, the flowers, the plantlife, the animals, the insects, the rivers—are vibrating and resounding with this great Song of Being. And all of these individual notes embodied by the forest seek to harmonize with the greatest, loudest and all encompassing Sound: *I AM.*

This is God's Spirit, or Divine Consciousness.

The Hidden Kingdom

So in this way, we can begin to imagine through the natural world this Hidden Kingdom in which we dwell.

We are One with God, and God is One with us, and what we perceive as the physical world through our bodies is truly a world of energy, and behind that world of energy, is a world of consciousness, and the nature of consciousness is truly a symphony of primordial music.

It is formless, and yet, sustains all forms.
All of life, and indeed, the entire cosmos, is Music.
It is one great ocean of vibrating essence,
resonating throughout and beyond time and space,
to a singular pure, perfect Note of unity.
And this Unity is the essence of Divine Love.

In some spiritual traditions, this pure and perfect pitch is called God. In others, it's called the Tao, or the Self, or Reality.

It is the One to which all life attains.
And although we are deaf to this Sound,
which resides on the deeper and higher levels of Reality,
it is resonating at all times within your Spirit,
for it is the sustainer of Life,
the primal Force and first mover of the Universe,
the Source from which all Being begins.

You, too, are part of this symphony.

The Harmony in Nature

It is through this harmony that we perceive beauty.
It is through this harmony that we perceive right and
  wrong.
Through this unity, we gain wisdom,

self acceptance, inner balance and peace.
From this Source of Life,
the creative energies flow,
and all abundance, and all knowledge.
By merging into this unity,
we come to know the nature of Life itself.
It comes from within, because We are That.

So when trying to understand the great unity of our existence, as perceived through the harmony of the natural world, know that God's Perfect Spirit or Consciousness is like a Song that all life is harmonizing to. It pervades all of existence. It is the backbone of matter and energy, and in fact, this Song is True Reality. It dwells within you, and you dwell within It. Each of us, a divine note in this great harmony of existence, all arising to the purest and greatest note of all, whose resonant quality is that of Pure Divine Love.

This means that all that we do in love harmonizes with the One, and from that, Life grows.

And since you are That, it is in fact uncovering our true nature, when we live and dwell within Love.

Listening to the Song

Although all life in this world is harmonizing with the One, it is difficult for us to do if we can't hear the Song. We are so small, so limited within the body, we do not hear it without listening through the heart with immense practice and discipline.

And so think of every person like a bell.
You are like a bell.
You are always ringing,
sending out vibrations of soul
that are invisible
and yet travel across
the ocean of God's spirit.
When we hold chaos inside of us—
pain, trauma, unresolved issues,
behavioral issues, selfishness, coldness—
we create a clanging, cacophonic sound
that ceases to harmonize with the One.
That is where all suffering arises.
It arises from our own discordant heart,
caused by our own ignorance
and inability to hear God's Song.
That Song resonates within the heart
clearer and clearer
as the heart becomes pure.
That Song is the Word, the Truth, and the Way.
It lives in you, and you can know it
through cultivating Love.

This is simply the nature of Life.

In order to hear the Song and clarify our spirit, we must practice perfect Love, and this brings us into harmony with God. Through our pure intentions, which leads to acts of merit, we become pure. It begins within our will—to become like the One, this perfect Song which all life attains to. And from the will arises our thoughts. And through purification of our thoughts, grows deepening devotion and desire to know Him. And from our desire, we work in service to mankind, and become a servant to all Life.

The Great Mirror

PERCEIVING LIFE THROUGH THE LENS OF
TRUTH

A great mystery of this Hidden Kingdom is found within the play of light and shadow.

Light and shadow define our earthly existence.

What is illuminated by day becomes obscure at night.

We see Light as purity and clarity. And so, we associate daylight with goodness and virtue.

Deeds done during the night, which remains in shadow, are deemed untrustworthy and unknowable.

Therefore, we say darkness is ignorance, and beneath the veil of night lurks evil.

As Within, So Without

In the Hidden Kingdom,
  the Light within is the Light throughout.
  The darkness within is the darkness throughout.

Here resides one of the mysterious laws of the Hidden Kingdom: we actually have two sets of eyes. One set, which we are most familiar with, are eyes of the flesh. There is no greater pleasure than gazing into the eyes of the one you love. You can sometimes tell the character of a person through their eyes; they are like windows to the soul. And we know our own eyes very well, we see them in the mirror every day. We know their color: blue or brown or green. We might be nearsighted or farsighted and wear glasses, too. Our eyes crinkle when we smile, and they wink when we're feeling mischievous. They remain open during the day when we are awake, and they close at night while we are sleeping. And so these are our first set of eyes, our physical eyes, and our vision is molded by them.

But we also have a secret set of eyes, and these are the eyes of the soul.

Our secret eyes are spiritual eyes that reside within our heart. For most of us, we are born with our spiritual eyes closed, and so we are unaware of them. But these eyes open with the inward illumination of the soul. And many people call this a *spiritual awakening*, when our soul's eyes begin to open.

Just as when we gaze into a mirror with our physical eyes and see our face, and we recognize ourselves outwardly in a human way, so in order to see God's

Spirit, our spiritual eyes must gaze into the mirror of the heart.

Through this inner illumination, we can truly know ourselves as Children of God, even as we are fully known. Then all mysteries are revealed.

Sin, blindness and ignorance
are not places we are meant to stay.
Just as day transitions into night,
so night transitions into day.

So within this play of light and shadow, what is dark can become illuminated, what is hidden can be unveiled, what is shrouded in darkness can be seen with clarity and Truth.

And once the pure Light of God's Spirit is seen through our spiritual eyes, the world becomes fully illuminated, and there is no more darkness. This means we see with more than just our physical eyes. Greater things enter into our perception than simply colors, shapes or movements. *We can see the Light Unchangeable: that great Spirit that pervades the world.* And as we open our spiritual eyes, we receive higher knowledge as well.

To receive this inner illumination, we must polish the mirror of the Heart.

The Mirror of the Heart

The heart is a great mirror, but when we are born into a human body, the mirror is cloudy and dark. It is like glass blackened by smoke. Like a lantern without a flame. And so the world seems like an endless maze, a labyrinth, empty of meaning or higher truth.

Due to the darkened mirror the heart, and our spiritual state of blindness, we are unaware of our true nature. We do not have clear perception of things. And so we stumble about in fear of a chaotic world, with poor discernment. We cannot tell night from day, evil from good, ignorance from righteousness. We move each way the wind blows, following wherever the crowd might lead us, lost but for a maze of endless desires.

The more we live in the world, filling our mind with materialism and our heart full of cravings, the more we suffer, the darker we become.

As little fireflies, we move from dark to light to dark again, uncomprehending of the Great Mirror, as the chaos within our heart is reflected in our lives.

Knowing the mirror is dark, we must polish it, and so this is why we take up a spiritual practice. We seek to purify the heart through acts of higher Love. Adopting a practice of loving-kindness toward all people, rooted in devotion to this great Spirit of Life, is the fastest and truest way to polish the mirror of the heart.

"Suppose there is a bowl of water covered over with plants and algae. If a man with good sight were to examine his own facial reflection in it, he would neither know nor see it as it really is. So too, when one dwells with a mind obsessed and oppressed by laziness, torpor, ill will, restlessness and worry."
~The Numerical Discourses of the Buddha

Through spiritual practice, we gain discipline over our mind and emotions, and we disentangle ourselves from troublesome behaviors. By following a faith, practice or sadhana, we untie the knots of our own blindfold.

"Now we see but a dim reflection as in a mirror; then we shall see face-to-face. Now I know in part; then I

shall know fully, even as I am fully known."
1 Corinthians 13:12

Slowly, our capacity to love deepens. Through a million small sacrifices of love, we let go, and our heart opens. Through grief, through trial, through hardship, through parenthood, we detach from the material world and become rooted in our spiritual conviction. We dedicate ourselves to the practice of highest Love. Our heart shines brighter and brighter. The mind becomes very pure, very virtuous, very self-forgetful. Our nature becomes very gentle, very calm, yet very courageous. And we come to seek God in all that we do.

Then comes the day of our Illumination.

The whole body becomes filled with Light, and we enter into the Hidden Kingdom.

When the heart becomes illuminated with God's light,

so that light is reflected within the Mind,

and our eyes are illuminated as well.

Then we can see Him. Darkness moves to Light. Knowledge previously hidden to us, obscured by the veil of our own ignorance, is unveiled and seen directly.

Then we see that the pure heart is the Kingdom, and the world around us is a Great Mirror.

Right View and Wrong View

The law of all spiritual practice is this: as within, so without.

Therefore, with great humility, we must self-reflect on how we live each day. We must accept there is a "right view" and a "wrong view" of how to live in this world.

The "wrong view" keeps us in darkness and suffering.

The "right view" guides us into higher joy, liberation and the light of the Hidden Kingdom.

Given to us through special revelation, the "right view" is rooted in the practice of virtue, for the illumined mind is a virtuous mind, and the illumined heart is a virtuous heart. From this comprehension of the "right view" proceeds the Way.

The "wrong view" truly lends itself to suffering and spiritual blindness—existing within a body, yet internally dead to the true Life. And this comes from pursuing materialistic and superficial gains, living under the sway of the ego, or finding ourselves in a mindset of "sin." And so this shadow blinds us and holds us bound, as though under the wings of a great dragon, trapping us in bondage. There is no greater Hell than the torture of one's own mind, the aching emptiness of the shuttered heart, and the perceived absence of our spiritual nature.

Therefore, understand that those who do evil live in this Night, their spiritual eyes closed, and they know not what they do. They are in suffering, perhaps so cold and numb, they do not comprehend themselves. The only blessing is that they cannot know what they remain blind to, and so their spiritual ignorance is like an armor donned against the Hell that they inhabit. Their hardness injures everyone that comes close, most deeply themselves. As illuminated Children of God, we must strive to forgive and tolerate as much darkness in others as we can, for within even the most wicked person resides the glimmer of God's Spirit, and the heart is never beyond redemption.

The Illuminated Mind

Creating a luminous mind leads to purification of the heart. And there is no higher illumination of the mind than dwelling on pure thoughts of loving-kindness, devotion and gratitude toward the Divine.

Likewise, purification of the heart gives rise to a luminous mind. And there is no purer heart than she or he who has been awakened to that Power, Creativity, Joy and Love Divine, who knows the Presence of one's God: the Reality within.

Just as the sun shines on a flower and it opens, so the illuminated mind shines upon the virtuous heart and it opens. The two arise as one.

And then we see that the world is a mirror: all of Life within my Heart, and my Heart within all Life.

Therefore, what you do to another, you do to yourself. What you say to another, you say to yourself. What you think of another, you think of yourself. And this explains the law of the prophets: "Treat others the way you want to be treated."

If you wish for the world to be generous to you, then be generous with the world by cultivating a generous mind. If you wish the world to be kind to you, then be kind to the world by cultivating a loving heart. If you wish for mercy, be merciful. If you wish for protection, then protect. If you wish for forgiveness, then forgive. And if you wish for success, then put your mind to it and work hard!

And so cultivation of a pure mind and a virtuous heart should take precedence above our bodily vanity or storing up "treasures of the earth" (Matt 6:19).

Understanding the world is a mirror, remember that a strong Mind benefits the world and leads to a strong body.

A weak Mind harms the world and leads to a weakened body.

Our thoughts come alive. There is no barrier between internal and external.

Ignorance and Illumination begins and ends with our mindset.

We must live this way if we wish to live in truth. This means we carry the burden of accountability for all of our actions, our thoughts, our behaviors, our suffering. I have no one to blame but me. And yet, in that, there is freedom. For if the burden of my actions rests solely upon my own shoulders, then I also hold the key to my liberation in hand.

The body is the opposite of what the soul is. It must be.

For a thing to see itself, it must first see what it is not. To know itself, know what it is not. And so residing in darkness we only know what we are not, identify as we are not, behave as we are not only seeing what we are not. We sacrifice what we are not to receive what we are. Every time the body breaks, the soul grows brighter. The unveiling of the heart gives rise to a flower of a thousand petals. The illumined mind becomes the lantern revealing the Way. Our true body, eternal, unending, is seen by gazing into the mirror of the pure heart.

The Silence of God

RISING INTO PRESENCE

All of Creation began in Silence.
In stillness, the Presence rises like a wave.
In solitude, we enter that deep oasis
in the heart; we sink a little more each day
until we strike upon the font of joy,
pure water flowing upward like a spring.
Rejoice! The Spirit fills us, wordless
but for a gasp of Love.

The Hidden Kingdom is an oasis of peace within the heart. In silence and stillness, we come to know that Presence that is greater than our own. In emptiness, we are filled with the Spirit of the Lord.

The Silence of God

Within silence, the seed of faith grows.

As we purify our hearts through spiritual living, it is important to understand the significance of the Silence of God.

When the heart opens through inward illumination, and we receive union with that Holy Spirit, we discover

176

a vast and endless ocean of silence within us, that is the purity of God's Presence.

In this silence, we can sink and sink and restore our soul. It heals the mind; it is a boon to the spirit. We are restored by this peace and inner tranquility.

Within silence and stillness, all of nature sinks into a meditative state of joy. With time, as we grow in Love and understanding, we no longer wish to speak very often of everyday things, or waste our words on gossip, current events or frivolous topics.

The mind, when occupied by these high and pure thoughts of God, has a tendency to drift upward and reside above the vocal chords, toward the crown of the head. This drifting upward is a peaceful, joyful, buoyant state (sometimes called "blissful.") We feel ourselves lifted into a constant state of grace. When the heart is illuminated with God's Spirit, the mind floats upward throughout the day, particularly when we enter into solitude and silence with Him, and we only wish to dwell in that pure space that resists all words, where the soul is One with Her God.

Simple

I am but a silent soul,
with secrets that escape all worlds,
and so I travel, life to life
to give my gifts, as you are owed.

I'd like to gift you with a heart,
and eyes that might see through this dream,
for all we lose are shadows
of our true, unrivaled vibrancy;

and the words I try to speak with,
all the methods that I use,
in the end, I am a simple Truth:
I give everything out of Love for you.

Sacred Inheritance

BORN FROM LOVE

What have I to fear when the Lord is with me?
What have I to fear when the Lord of Love calls?

    He's faith
    and courage
    and hope aplenty!
    What have I to fear
    when I serve my God?

Sing to the night, the Lord is with me!
Sing to the night, the Lord of Love calls!

    He's faith
    and courage
    and hope aplenty . . .
    What have I to fear
    when I serve my God?

    Good morning, little God.

I would like to remind you today that you were born from Love, and this Love preceded the universe.

And if you find that you are living in fear, there are a few reasons for that.

The first being that you have forgotten your native state, which is that of the Lord of Love.

The second being . . . that you must trust in God.

You Will Never Be Separated

We hear it said in many different traditions that we must trust in God, that we must have faith.

Indeed, more blessed are the ones who have faith and yet do not see Him.

And so today, I want to reassure you, little God, that there are those who can see Him, and there are many who have, and what might feel like a great, dark abyss of existence to you is filled to the brim with Life.

The very Spirit of Life is at all times resonating and singing throughout every atom in existence, sustaining all of this.

And if you think of how big it is . . .

How big is this universe! How big is your heart! How big is the Tree of Life?

If you think of the size of it, the magnitude.

And then, even if you take just a small slice of it, maybe just a single leaf from a tree, you can take that leaf and you can cut that into little pieces and you can look at those pieces, and you'll see even smaller pieces inside of that.

And it goes on and on and on, endlessly, infinitely.

And all of this is to reassure you, little soul, that your presence here is not a mistake.

It is not by any sort of accident that you have found me, that I have found you.

In fact, I am trying to lead you back to your sacred Heart, that you might remember who you are, and that you are indeed the creator of things, the knower of things, the lover of things.

And what is fear to such a God?

What is fear to such a Creator that lives inside of you?

What is fear, when you have the power to manifest your entire existence?

And these bonds that we live in—they are just bonds of the mind. They're just little shackles we put on ourselves, little labels we use to limit ourselves. Because if we understood the infinity of our own existence, we would escape this body instantly, and run off and play in the stars.

And perhaps that is what many of us are doing now.

So I want to reassure you, my love, that no one has ever died. They have simply stepped into the next room. No one has ever ceased to exist. You have always existed.

Nothing in this life is by chance.

It is all dictated by the state of your heart.

And if you seek freedom, if you seek liberation, if you want the path out of this suffering, it is inside of you. You are in complete control.

And in fact, it is your destiny to discover this inheritance at the heart of yourself, to learn of your true nature, little god: that all of life is at all times organizing itself around you in a galaxy full of potential.

You are the creator of things. You are the artist, you are the musician, you are the writer, you are the engineer. And don't forget: Love is the highest Master.

And so today, little soul, let us set aside this shadow of fear and take heart, for we serve a God of Love.

And remember that you are His child. You are indeed the heart of His existence, and He is the heart of yours, and you have nothing to fear, for you are One with the Eternal.

About the Author
THERESA LORRAINE

*I*t   *is*   *True:*

Love   *is*   *the*   *Path,*
the   *path*   *is*   *You.*

I am a spiritual writer, a poet and independent scholar. Many people are looking for evidence of God, or answers about the nature of the divine. My goal is to encourage you to embrace a spiritual life without fear.

I experienced a profound illumination at 12 years old that has since been validated by the Vedanta Society of Seattle, WA, as "Self-Realization" or "Self-Illumination." In Christian tradition, this amazing experience of God's Presence is called a "baptism in the Holy Spirit." I have spent my life learning about how this incredible experience of God is witnessed in major religions and sacred traditions. I have practiced with Buddhists, Christians, spiritualists, agnostics and everything in between. I do not discriminate between faiths, but have been a student of Theology,

Anthropology and philosophy my entire life. My humble mission is to serve you by shedding light upon the beautiful Truth that exists at the heart of all religions.

We are all One in the Tree of Life.

Follow Online

Medium   –
https://treeoflifespirituality.medium.com/

Youtube   –
*https://www.youtube.com/@treeoflife_spiritua
lity*

*You can read more about my life and spiritual
experiences in my memoir entitled:
"SPIRITUAL" by Theresa Lorraine.*

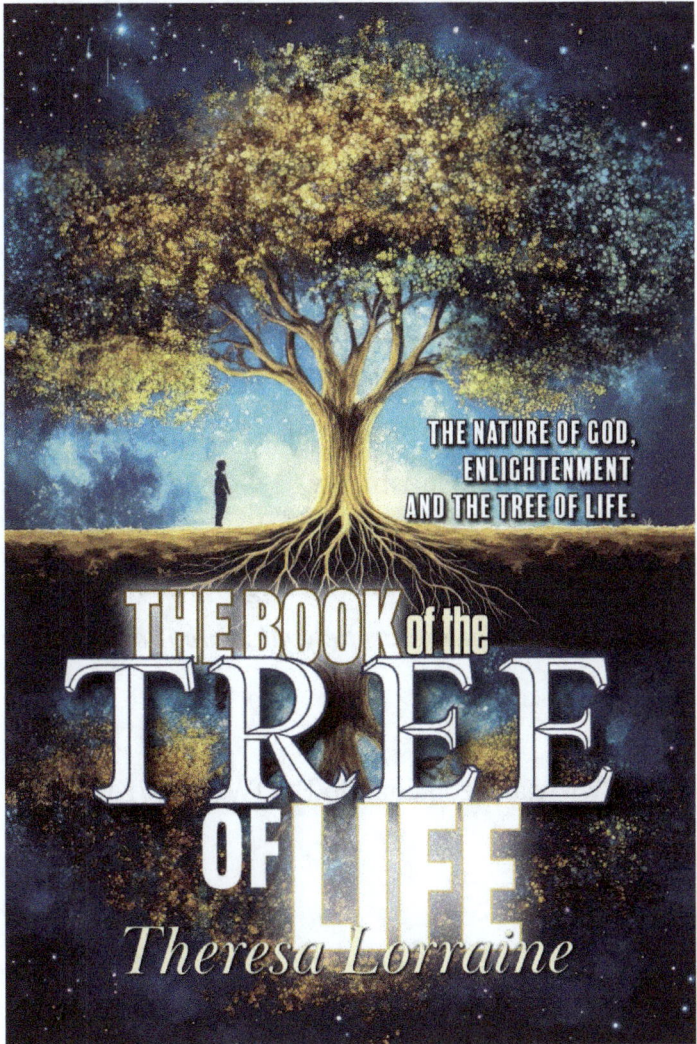

THE NATURE OF GOD,
ENLIGHTENMENT
AND THE TREE OF LIFE.

THE BOOK of the
TREE
OF LIFE

Theresa Lorraine

The Book of the Tree of Life is an exploration of the deepest spiritual truths found in religious mysticism: the nature of God, Self and the spiritual path. In a friendly and heartwarming conversation, Theresa Lorraine draws a string of truth through three intersecting points of world religions: the nature of God, the nature of Enlightenment, and the archetype of the Tree of Life. She includes commentary on the spiritual practice of Kabbalah, Sufism, Hinduism, Buddhism, Christianity and more.

Let us explore the intersecting harmony of all religions through the archetypal symbol of the Tree of Life.

https://www.amazon.com/dp/B0DWQWT7KC

Are you seeking the Tree of Life?

SPIRITUAL

a memoir

THERESA LORRAINE

At 12 years old, Theresa Lorraine experiences an Awakening that will change her life, and reform her understanding of God and Reality. Through vivid poetry and personal diary entries, this book contains Theresa's firsthand account of seeing God's Spirit manifest within and throughout the natural world as a Presence and Consciousness that transcends all human comprehension. From grief to love to spiritual Enlightenment, Theresa openly shares her life spent in service to the One, from being orphaned as a young adult, to arriving at the greatest of all Revelations: we are all One in the Tree of Life.

Tree of Life Spiritual Podcast

I invite you to listen to me speak about spirituality, meditation, prayer, the philosophy of the Tree of Life and the unity of religions.

Youtube
https://www.youtube.com/@treeoflife_spirituality

Spotify
http://podcasters.spotify.com/pod/show/treeoflifes pirituality

Substack
https://substack.com/@treeoflifespirituality

Find Me on Social Media

Medium Blog
https://medium.com/@treeoflifespirituality

Instagram
https://www.instagram.com/treeoflife_spirituality

Tiktok
https://www.tiktok.com/@treeoflife_spirituality

www.ingramcontent.com/pod-product-compliance
Lightning Source LLC
LaVergne TN
LVHW021121080426
835513LV00011B/1189